go **girl**

go **girl**

finding adventure wherever your travels lead

marlee LeDai

illustrated by Leyah Jensen

Revell
Grand Rapids, Michigan

Text © 2005 by Marlee LeDai
Illustrations © 2005 by Leyah Jensen

Published by Revell Books
a division of Baker Publishing Group
P.O. Box 6287, Grand Rapids, MI 49516-6287

Printed in the United States of America

Library of Congress Cataloging-in-Publication Data
LeDai, Marlee, 1948–
    Go girl : finding adventure wherever your travels lead / Marlee LeDai ;
illustrated by Leyah Jensen.
        p.   cm.
    Includes bibliographical references.
    ISBN 0-8007-5971-0 (pbk.)
    1. Travel—Religious aspects—Christianity. 2. Christian pilgrims and pilgrim-
ages. 3. Women travelers—Religious life. 4. Christian women—Religious life.
I. Title.
BV5067.L43 2005
263′.041—dc22   2004027256

To Tirza, Leyah, Lissa, Mira, and Annah.
You are my greatest adventure yet.

Contents

7

Travel brings a special kind of wisdom if one is open to it. At home or abroad, things of the world pull us toward them with such gravitational force that, if we are not alert our entire lives, we can be sucked into their outwardness. Attentive travel helps us to see this, because the continually changing outward scene helps us to see through the world's pretensions ... the world loses its wager.

Huston Smith

Start Packing

A Trip Is a Way to Amaze Yourself

The year I graduated from college, the era of flower power and lava lamps, I bought a one-way ticket from L.A. to London. I packed a bag with a sweater and a couple of pointy-collared shirts—all I needed to go with the jeans on my hips and the boots on my feet. My plane was the last to arrive at a then-tiny suburban airport, way past dark and miles from a tube station. Other travelers quickly jumped into the few available taxis. No one from the guest house in Essex where I'd arranged to work showed up to fetch me. Buzzing from jet lag, I was alone and bewildered.

But I had thrown down a challenge to life. Setting out to seek my fortune in the wide world, I was determined not to go home again until I had found it. For the next two years—on the move across Britain, Europe, and the Middle East—my odysseys were lived as holy questions. And like the historical saint Ignatius, who encouraged young Jesuits to go on pilgrimage without food, money, or creature comforts, I was interested not in how much I could see and do but in an encounter with amazing grace.

"The pilgrimage was an invitation to experience openness, wonder and dependence on the strange ways in which God provides," explains Australian priest Michael McGirr of Ignatius. The point was "to see how grateful he could become."[1]

Do you want to be in tutelage under God's holy and often raucous imagination?

Issue an invitation to yourself. Confront the limitations of your soul. Defiantly provoke the certitudes of everyday life. Take a trip. Go somewhere. Anywhere. Go where nothing matters but the adventure. "We are all strangers in this world," writes Phil Cousineau, "and part of the elusive wonder of travel is that during those moments far away from all that is familiar, we are forced to face that truth . . . of our soul's journey here on earth."[2]

Nearly everyone dreams of a trip to Paris or Hawaii. Many of us make that kind of romantic pilgrimage at least once in our lifetimes. Perhaps you crave the more exotic: to trek in Tibet with a sherpa guide or to stand atop Jerusalem's ancient citadel. Does the glitz of New York City call to you? The colorful carefree spirit of Mexico? The austere grandeur of Alaska's waterways and glaciers? Or do you simply want a peaceful day at the seashore listening to the surf? Even if you're up for just a hike around the block, this book is written for you. It is not about taking dream vacations. It is not about luxury cruises, whirlwind tours to glamorous cities, or the best hotels. This book is about the adventure that is already within you.

Explore this earth and you'll uncover soul terrain, wherever the road leads. The landscape you see and the circumstances you encounter may differ greatly each trip, but the result will always be the same. Travel is about a shift in perspective, a shift that just might change how you see and what you expect from life itself. This is a book about challenging the everydayness of the familiar, volunteering to become a stranger for a time in order to meet yourself.

It is also a book about *being* the adventure as much as seeking it. It is about what happens when you put on your traveling shoes and head out to discover the unexpected. Even a business trip can become a sacred journey.

Can you see already that a trip is a way to amaze yourself with your own energy, resilience, and spontaneity?

You will.

Of course, you may suffer indigestion, motion sickness, or lumpy mattresses. You're sure to find long lines at the check-in counter and rude officials at the screening box. You may lack the money to do what you've planned for or dreamed of at your destination—or run out of it far too quickly. But I've found that the most interesting travels are those on which I had little to spend. The best destinations were those dependent upon the resources of my own consciousness. The greatest hindrance to a great trip is lack of imagination.

When I boarded that TWA airplane right out of college, I had a hundred dollars in my pocket. My goal was not peripheral, however, but visceral. I wanted to test my grit, my gumption, my gut-level knowing. I would encounter plenty of opportunity.

Before I returned home two years later, I had worked in a home for the mentally unbalanced in England, a pension in Austria, a peanut farm in Israel, and an evangelistic community in Germany. For good or bad (and one of those places was very bad), my pilgrimage brought me wisdom and gave me a sense of power to do and be—gifts that were bequeathed not from the outside in but from the inside out. These gifts would surface at the most surprising moments, when I felt fragile or weakened. Huston Smith, professor of religion and philosophy at Syracuse University, explains that the art of travel "is to learn to master today's unavoidable situation with as much equanimity as we can muster, in preparation for facing its sequel tomorrow."[3]

A journey, after all, is a metaphor for life. When I leave home for any reason, I live this metaphor right out loud. A trip anywhere means struggling with my perceived inadequacies juxtaposed against perpetual wonder. This is so for the intriguing people I meet too: the forty-something backpacker who started traveling to out-of-the-way places when her husband left her for a "pop-tart." The thirty-something chick who set out for foreign shores after watching her mother die too young. The seventy-something retired army officer who, via bus, was finally seeing the country he had defended and served.

You can fly high or take the low road. Board a cruise ship to the Bahamas or a kayak on the Boa River. Trek the entire Pacific Crest Trail or just a stretch of it. Do a home exchange with a family from another country. Choose the backroads, backwoods, or backseat. Cut your own trail to a natural hot spring in the Pacific Northwest or mingle with tourists speaking every language at the Great Wall of China. Travel by yourself or with a group, for a weekend, a fortnight, or a year. Travel to a place you've never been or a place you've been a thousand times.

The thing is—go. Just go and seek excitement or respite, entertainment or your own beautiful thoughts.

Perhaps you've never been out of state or out of town. Perhaps you've been hit with financial losses, the loss of a companion, or the loss of a dream to visit Timbuktu. (Yes, it really is a place, and I once met a fellow who'd been there just to say he had!) Perhaps you've aged or have been saddled with an illness, a physically challenged child, or an irrational fear of flying. You say there are far more reasons to stay home than there are to go? You see the obstacles, the myriad details impossible to plan? You're worried about everything that can go wrong?

Remember, each one of us is already on a fabulous journey, the trip of a lifetime. We are, after all, strangers on this earth, on our way to a place we've never been before. Ours is an open-ended journey, and there is no turning back. But travel as adventure is about recognizing that the road will rise up to meet you and me as we keep putting one foot in front of the other. In this book, we'll explore what happens when, as pilgrims, we make our way to the promised land. We're going to build some altars at the turning points in our journey. We're going to scout out the valleys, taste their sweet wine, and build bridges strong enough for those who come after us.

You'll never see the sea divide with your own eyes until you take the first step. So pick up your skirts, drop your pretensions, and shake your tambourines.

I'll see you on the other side.

Part 1

An Encounter
with Amazing Grace

1

HerStory

Women on the Go

Do you realize you are a woman and cannot go just anywhere?

Abba Arsenius to a female pilgrim, fifth century

The market is suddenly recognizing the power of the adventuress. The chicks are the future of the industry.

abcnews.go.com

Zoe's brown eyes sparkled when I bumped into her at the grocery store. "I've been invited on a trip to Turkey," she told me. "My boss has offered the time off. But how can I leave my work this time of year?"

"There's never a good time," I told my twenty-one-year-old friend. "Just go—before you've twice as many reasons to stay."

Although for me, career, family, and age have made traveling inconvenient and impractical, I'm still taking my own advice. I wonder about where I will go next and think back to my first real journey. I was about Zoe's age—touring Europe with my sister in

1970. I'll admit now what I knew intuitively then: everyone travels alone. No matter who accompanies you, any trip is an interior one. It will affect you as it does no other. The thing that makes a journey distinctly individual is what you bring to it from within yourself.

By putting yourself in a place you've never been before, you reveal yourself to yourself, says Thalia Zepatos, who writes about the hows, whys, and wherefores of journey. That's what travel industry gurus claim motivates female travelers. As opposed to men, who venture out in search of "external observation," women on the go are seeking personal epiphanies. A woman traveling alone is no longer any kind of novelty, claims Evelyn Hamon, creator of journeywoman.com. Research shows we make 70 percent of all travel decisions and are a hardy bunch. Seventy-five percent of those who take nature, adventure, or cultural trips are women; the average adventure traveler is a forty-seven-year-old female who wears a size twelve dress. These women spent fifty-five billion dollars on outdoor equipment in 2003.[1]

Websites geared to women who travel proliferate on the Internet. They document the trend with names that range from the holy, such as sacredjourneys.com, to the whimsical, like bootsnall. com. These sites spawn yet more popular travel-for-women newsletters that reach thousands of subscribers each month. In other travel news since 2000, Delta launched its own hip airline, Song, to lure female travelers. This is appropriate, for solo pilot Amelia Earhart shocked society in the 1920s by suggesting air travel would become as commonplace as trips by train. A daredevil, she set a standard maintained today by women astronauts.

Who could know how far we'd go?

The best way to make your dreams come true is to wake up.

Paul Valery

Since prehistoric eras when women wandered as nomads, moving in tribes, our place in the world has been shaped by the gumption of spirited women who have dared to act of their own volition. A servant named Hagar was one of the earliest female travelers whose story and name are documented.

When Hagar conceived a baby by her mistresses's husband, she fled harsh treatment by hitting the trail. Far from community, she intended to forage for herself and by herself. In one of history's most poignant records, an otherworldly being found her weary and despondent. Comforted by this presence, Hagar addressed the divine as "the-God-Who-Sees."[2] Since that time, women who dare to act on behalf of their own souls have experienced grace in the world and have seen its hidden beauty through the eyes of the-God-Who-Sees.

Later in Hebrew history, Abigail, a woman of pure moxie, showed again a female's ability to pick up and go when it makes sense. When her community was threatened, Abigail "made haste" to load donkeys with two hundred loaves of bread, two skins of wine, five sheaths of roasted grain, a hundred clusters of raisins, and two hundred cakes of figs. Then she set off on her own donkey—to meet the pursuing warriors, not to flee from them. Her courage to ride out into enemy territory won her admiration, and in time, she basically won the lottery of the day: she became the wife of Israel's good king David.[3]

Little is known about female disciples who traveled like the apostles during the first century. According to a story told in a second-century manuscript, however, the daughter of a leading citizen of Iconium, Turkey, declared herself a Christian and was condemned to burn at the stake. Disguising herself as a man, Thecla ran to another city after a rain shower put out the fire. When captured again, she escaped the wild beast show at the local amphitheater and ran off to who knows where. As she moved from town to town, Thecla became a miracle healer and

19

Why Water Keeps You Going

Glow about town more. Drinking plenty of water is the best and least expensive way to make skin appear luminous. (Makers of cosmetics won't give away this secret.)

Stop dehydration, which can cause fuzzy thought processes, short-term memory lapses, and focusing difficulties—not good when traveling. Plane travel, especially, can dehydrate. But a bottle of water keeps you fresh. Sure, this creates more trips to the lavatory, but ask for an aisle seat and show off your outfit!

PASSPORT

Shut down hunger pangs with a glass of water. I often mistake thirst for hunger anyway; don't you?

Ease achy bones when in a damp climate by drinking a glass of water—though you may be tempted to drink hot tea. Keep in mind: caffeine in any form (including tea and colas) dehydrates. If you simply can't do without caffeine's jolt, try to drink at least one glass of water for every cup of caffeine.

Some Water Tips for Your Travels:

Meet your water quota by eating a juicy or fibrous piece of fruit or vegetable when drinking plenty of water presents a challenge.

Beware that all bottled water is not pure or "spring" derived. Overseas some bottled water is simply local tap water sold at high prices for travelers. Always buy a known brand sold at larger markets, and stock up if going to remote areas.

Carry a Nalgene bottle, sold at sporting goods stores or travel shops, and refill it where water is safe for drinking; the bottle will not allow bacteria to grow.

shared her faith with many. Her dauntlessness as a woman on the move is our legacy.[4]

Above all else, you must make the decision to overcome inertia. Every reason not to travel was written on the wind.

Rob Sangster

As Christianity became established in the fourth century, Empress Helena, mother of Constantine, traveled widely in the Holy Land, mingling with ordinary folks. Her desire to worship at the places touched by Jesus preserved the sites before the onslaught of crusaders could wipe them out. Helena's visits to Bethlehem, Mount Sinai, Golgotha, and the Mount of Olives resulted in churches being built there. These structures protected the sacred ground for generations of pilgrims. Though wealth bought her the privilege of travel, Helena distributed clothing and money to the poor and dressed as they did. Her sightseeing became our mutual heritage.[5]

But in the Middle Ages, at the height of pilgrimage, St. Benedict denounced—for monks and women—this wandering about to holy sites. "Inappropriate mobility" was thought to lead to immorality and to degenerate into mere tourism. In the eighth century, St. Boniface advised the archbishop of Canterbury to prevent matrons and "veiled women" (nuns) from making frequent pilgrimage. Not long after, legislation was passed forbidding it. The law framed the prohibition as a declaration setting women "free from the necessities of travel."[6] Who did they think they were kidding? Women continued to be the most devout and eager to embark on this form of spiritual adventure. Today, medieval English theater is famed for its concern with redemption and the paradigm of walking as a redemptive activity.

The Tradition of the Adventuress

At home in England, women of the Victorian era couldn't go to the British museum without a chaperone. Yet during the same era, there were those who, each known as an "adventuress," traveled solo to isolated and exotic parts of the world. Later, American women joined their ranks, models of feminine ingenuity and spunk:

Isabella Bird, daughter of a clergyman, left England at age twenty-two for America's Rocky Mountains. Bird covered a thousand miles, mostly by horseback in winter, writing her way through rugged terrain. It's said that her ink froze as she wrote.

Gertrude Bell set off to make her mark in the Middle East when she didn't marry as expected of her. In becoming an ally of Lawrence of Arabia and advisor to Iraq's King Faisal, she made a place for herself as statesman for British interests in Tehran.

Freya Stark traveled through Persia and settled in Baghdad, setting out to remote areas on foot and by donkey cart. She created an anti-Nazi propaganda network for the Allied Forces along the way.

Mary Henrietta Kingsley, an ethnologist, was the first woman to enter parts of Africa. She traversed much country that had been completely unknown. She traveled on foot and by canoe, recording her observations of wildlife as well as culture.

Harriet Chalmers Adams was regarded as the foremost woman explorer of her time. At age fourteen, she made a horseback journey with her father from Oregon to the Mexican border. Later, she told how it set her gypsy spirits dancing. She visited almost every Latin American country, and as a war correspondent for *Harper's* magazine during World War I, she was the only woman allowed to visit the trenches in France. She became the first president of the Society of Woman Geographers in 1925.

Nellie Bly, named the best American reporter of the Victorian era, traveled around the world in seventy-two days in 1889 to beat the fictional record of Jules Verne's character Phileas Fogg. Noted for her bravado, she also posed as an insane woman to report on life in a madhouse, as an unwed mother to expose the baby-buying trade, and as a thief to experience a night in jail.

Louise Arner Boyd was the world's foremost explorer of Arctic regions for over forty years. Beginning in 1931, she was involved in researching, photographing, and studying polar phenomena. Boyd was also the first woman to fly over the North Pole.

Even today, fear for the vulnerability of our bodies has limited women's access to the world. It continues to be a factor in how far we venture and whether we travel at all. Yet it has never stopped women's desire to participate with the-God-Who-Sees in the twin ideas of spiritual growth and adventure.

My pilgrim road has not been smooth, and I don't expect yours to be: I see this as a major benefit.

Jennifer Westwood

Ever heard of rough and tough women Vikings? In the tenth century, Gudridur sailed across frigid northern seas into the new world Leif Eriksson had discovered. There she gave birth to a son, the first European born on the American continent. There she became a widow when natives killed her husband. As a devotee of Jesus Christ, she later returned home and walked across the continent of Europe in order to offer a first person account of her voyage and experience. She's considered the most traveled woman of the Middle Ages.

Five hundred years later, eighteen women crossed the stormy Atlantic on a damp wooden ship. Two gave birth during the cold sixty-five-day journey from Holland to Plymouth. Only six of the women survived to the following spring, but their gumption generated a new world based on new ideas. Generations later, Americans laud their sacrificial journey with thanksgiving.

Since that time, America's women adventurers have shown the same kind of grit and moxie. These included Native Americans like Sacagawea, who gave birth while traversing the difficult passages of the Pacific Northwest in 1804. She guided a party of European male explorers, one her husband, and was praised as the inspiration and genius of their trek.

23

Not even half a century later, women from various ethnic backgrounds were propelled on a new kind of pilgrimage. Crossing two thousand miles of the most treacherous territory on the continent, they trudged by foot along the Oregon Trail, passing close to footprints left by Sacagawea. That the pioneers found it difficult beyond their wildest imaginings has been documented by scraps of journals and stories handed from mother to daughter. Many of the women who made this trek were not asked whether they wanted to go at all. Yet their tenacity under the worst of conditions has left an indelible mark on the history of women adventurers.

Don't think the Victorian era that followed was less audacious. Its prim domestic stereotype doesn't hold. Many young women were not content with society's expectations to marry well and raise families. The women's missionary movement characterized eagerness to embrace adventure. Predominantly single, two women for every man left America and England for the teeming cities of China, India, and Africa. Amy Carmichael, who rescued girls from temple prostitution, found the work difficult not least because of the loneliness inherent in it. "Lord, how can I go on to the end?" she prayed. Yet fifty years of ministry in India speaks for itself.[7]

Female adventurers of the modern era are numerous, and their stories fascinate (see sidebar on page 22). Their lives were often "more terrible than triumphant," say the editors of a fabulous book about them. The editors add that by traveling "fearlessly into the blank spaces on the map" these women "made comprehensible a part of the world that we didn't know, understand or appreciate."[8] Such women discoverers also made apparent the limitless capabilities of the human spirit.

The Power to Fly

The best online sites to help you plan your travels? *Consumer Reports* names these the big three: expedia.com, orbitz.com, and travelocity. com. Generally, you'll find the lowest fares for the most convenient route on travelocity.com, but always compare rates from site to site. Priceline. com and hotwire.com can offer incredible deals, but they don't offer services that let you know the airline or exact flying times until after you commit to buy a ticket. (The trick is to bid with an absurdly low figure the first time, because if your offer is accepted, you're obligated to buy the ticket. You're required to give a credit card number from the start.)

See also trip.com, cheaptickets.com, and lowestfare.com. If when visiting a ticket site you find a reasonable offer that suits your budget and schedule, your best bet is to buy it. The next time you open the same website, the offer may be gone or the price may be higher.

Specific airlines deals: The websites of specific airlines may offer better deals or more convenient flight times than both general online ticket sites and conventional ticket services. Check, as it pays to shop—buying tickets online can get you special fares or free miles.

Last-minute advantage: If you're traveling solo or don't have to be a particular place at a set time, flying standby is a great way to go—and begs for adventure. Flying standby may get you there sooner or later, and last-minute tickets can sometimes be had for a song. (Note: The only reputable company/site for standby flights is airtech.com. They even have a phone number on the website that you can call for information. A sample price for any one-way flight to Europe, for example, is $200, or for Hawaii $100.)

Niche advantage: Find websites for adventure travel, travel for women only, travel for singles, or certain types of travel like cruises by typing in key words on a search engine. You'll discover companies for the most unanticipated niches of travel, and you may be surprised by special deals or trips to places you'll love but have never heard of.

E-ticket advantage: In many airports you can skip the check-in line entirely by bringing carry-on baggage only and having a ticket ordered online. Get both ticket and boarding pass at self-service kiosks. Even if you do check luggage, e-tickets mean you're in the system—no worries about losing your ticket or paper tickets arriving late. An e-ticket is essentially a confirmation number that secures your seat (so record the number at least two places). You'll be asked to print out your receipt and itinerary and bring these with you to the airport. You may have to present the credit card with which you purchased your e-ticket.

Photo ID reminder: Always carry government-issued photo identification for check-in with any airline. You won't be allowed to fly without it. A secure zippered pouch that hangs around your neck and can be tucked inside a shirt is the best way I've found to carry driver's license, passport, credit card, and a little cash.

All places are alike to me because everywhere I expect to find God, who is the only object of all my desires.

St. Therese Couderc

After I graduated from college in the early 1970s, plans to travel with friends fell through when they changed their minds about going overseas. I didn't. I set out to seek my fortune alone, eventually finding myself in the Middle East. Living in Israel during the tense period between the Munich Olympic massacre (August 1972) and the Yom Kippur War (October 1973) was not exactly my idea of fun. The kind of trip I had in mind did not include what happened: being pelted with stones at a Palestinian camp in Gaza, hitchhiking through the Negev while fighter jets buzzed overhead, and inadvertently swimming with sharks in the Red Sea. I got more adventure than I bargained for. But that journey led beyond a Holy Land pilgrimage. It led me to a holy place within myself.

Since that time my path has not been clear-cut like the paved yellow brick road. During one particularly dark period in my life, I despaired. I could not identify the rocky place as a holy destination on my life map. Desperate for another epiphany twenty-five years after my first pilgrimage, I once again flung a backpack over my shoulder. This time I set out with my twenty-one-year-old daughter. We shared trains packed with gypsies and picnicked with alpine goats. We visited landmarks that had been special to me decades before. Yet spectacular cathedrals, beautiful works of art, and hoards of young travelers in Birkenstocks left me thinking, *Been there. Done that.*

While my daughter was making her own discoveries, not appropriating mine, I found myself wondering, *What will this trip reveal to me about myself?* We were in Paris the day of Princess Diana's sudden death when something struck me like a slow-motion crash in a dark tunnel. For years I had identified with

26

Princess Di, who was picking up the pieces after a divorce and moving on. I had watched with the world as she began her purpose all over again, reaching out to others and defining a brand-new mission. Just as her life was an inspiration to me, her death became an epiphany. It helped me rediscover, as a pilgrim, the holiest destination of all: not one of us knows how long we're going to live, but we do know how we ought to live—and we must dare to live that way, loving even at the risk of losing.

"Only you can tell your story," writes Whitney Otto in *How to Make an American Quilt*.[9] At times it takes a grand or reckless adventure to discover that. To make a journey is to multiply encounters with your own possibilities. Whether you are 21, 41, or 101 years old, let your pilgrimage begin. We've been given the legacy of female visionaries. These women challenged their own and their culture's limitations. In the face of formidable woes, they expanded the world.

So go with much money or barely any. Go in blue jeans or skirts. Go near or far, fast or slow, alone, with a friend, or with a group. Just go. Step out of those revolving doors, off the beaten track, and onto the road less traveled. Find some wonderful corner of the world and immerse yourself in it. Find out what you have to say to yourself.

My friend Zoe is doing this, so I will share with her my photographs of Turkey. I'll tell her how Istanbul's Blue Mosque looks in the pouring rain and describe the ruins of Ephesus awash in light on a summer night. I'll wonder what Zoe's personal epiphany will be. I'll encourage her to observe and reflect. I'll tell her, "Don't be surprised if when you get back you feel both less and more at home.

"Everything will be just as it was before," I'll add. "But you won't be."

Unpacking Western Africa

A Pilgrim's Profile: Christine Gilman

How I learned that courage is given me
to discover my life purpose and enable
me to give myself to it

No-one seeks God whom God is not calling. Pilgrims are people who have been evoked by someone or something to seek out the divine.

Jennifer Westwood, *Sacred Journeys*

One year after Christine Gilman traveled to Liberia to document the need for adoptive families, she returned to adopt a daughter of her own. Ama, four years old, weighed just twenty-nine pounds when she joined a family that included Christine's husband, Tim, and three older children. "It seems to me, we are either backing away from the thing we're meant to do or we're going toward it," she says now of the decision to get personally involved with the needs of others.

Meanwhile, civil war raged in Liberia. Christine, an artist and homemaker in Salem, Oregon, watched TV reports of seven Liberian women carrying Bibles down the streets of Monrovia. Dressed in white and wearing African headdresses, they stopped to speak to the world: "Kill us or not, we are going to stand and pray in public. We are tired of war and of seeing our sons killed. We are going to pray night and day until we have peace." This made a huge impression on Christine, who was safely back at home. She says, "War in Africa is not just about dying. It is about having your limbs and noses and private parts cut off and being left to bleed as an example to others."

About that time, rebel troops invaded Hoover Children's Village near Monrovia, where Ama had lived, terrorizing the 510 children (ages two to seventeen). In their wake, Liberia's military army arrived with AK-47s to search for the rebels, dismantling the compound. They stole what the rebels had left behind and threatened to kill the children before sending them into the jungle in the pouring rain.

Traumatized, the children trekked ten hours through swamps and marshes to the country's capital. In a bombed-out building, they lived for weeks on one tablespoon of rice per day. When the military moved on, the children marched back to their orphanage, finding nothing but walls of brick.

The miracle? Of the 510 children, not one was lost.

Within weeks, African Christian Fellowship International sent an email to supporters, asking for female volunteers from America to come to Liberia to comfort the children and help them start again. Orphanage founder, Ed Kofi, told potential volunteers, "We need you to be here right now more than we need food or money for rebuilding."

Christine had no doubts about responding. Admitting that kind of challenge fit what she calls her "spiritual shape," she says, "My daughter was once one of those children. How could I not go? Nothing was more important at that time than to give those kids a hug and a little bit of hope."

Christine bought her own ticket and within days met up with other volunteers in London. Then they flew to Accra, capital of Ghana and entry point to Liberia. "Accra was in no better shape than Liberia," she says. "With military coups there, the tension was overwhelming. At the airport, soldiers pointed their guns in our direction as we disembarked."

But with a sense of clarity, Christine encourages others to do the difficult thing when it is called for: "Don't be afraid to throw your hat in the ring. Our life is meant to expand as an expression of goodness. Every time we choose fear, we are backing ourselves into a dark corner. We are losing an opportunity. People think, *Oh, I'll just sit here and wait until I have the courage to go.* No. Courage requires you to stand up off your chair and walk toward it. If you're not doing the thing that requires courage, then you are siding with the darkness by the fact that you are not doing anything."

Christine lived out this viewpoint in planning how to pack for the trip also. She explains that before she left for Liberia, she knew she had to fill her bag with what the kids needed. She also knew that each visitor was only allowed to take in forty pounds, including carry-on. "That's the way they get money from you," she says, adding that she ignored the limits and packed two bags weighing eighty pounds each, and two thirty-five-pound carry-ons. They were filled with underwear, toys, medicine, hygiene products, and wooden toys. She also stuffed quite a few *People* magazines and twenty CDs into the pockets of her carry-on.

Standing in line in Ghana, Christine quickly calculated that her luggage was going to cost five hundred dollars in overweight fees. She says, "At the baggage counter, my heart was pounding. But I told myself, 'This is what the children need. I'm going to do what I have to do to take this in because I am standing with God.'"

"The baggage clerk had her little bifocals on, typing away. She didn't look at me," says Christine. "I began, 'Hello, I have some magazines your family would like—all about movie stars.' The clerk didn't look up but put forth her empty hand. I put in three or four magazines, then asked, 'Do you have a CD player?' She nodded yes, but still did not look at me even once. I added, 'I bet you have children; would you like Christian CDs?' She put out her hand again, typing away with the other one. Then she looked up at me, gave me a little smile, and said, 'You may go.' She loaded my bags and never punched in the weight!"

At the Children's Village, Christine met Mary, one of the orphanage supervisors, who told her about the day the rebels came. One of them had beaten Mary with his rifle until her blood flowed. Then he stripped her, looking for money in her body parts. All this, Christine reminds us, happened in front of the kids. Mary told Christine she had looked at the soldier and said, "Go ahead and kill me. I know who I am. I know who carries me. I know where I'm going. Don't just be a coward and beat me. Go ahead and kill me straight out. Go! Do it!"

"It's an amazing thing to meet women like Mary," says Christine. "The experience gives me courage every day."

"I will continue to take risks," Christine says. "I'm not going to be stupid about it, because I want to continue to live and to do good. But it seems that our work is to discover our life and to give ourselves to it with all our heart. We can't be in denial, because things are going to go wrong, things will be against us. We just have to face them and say, 'I'm going forward whether anyone else is with me or not. I'm going forward in the name of all that is good and all that is holy.'"

2

A Holy Calling

No Strings Attached

The trip had never been billed in my mind as an adventure in the sense of something to be proved. And it struck me then that the most difficult thing had been the decision to act, the rest had been merely tenacity—the fears were paper tigers. One really could do anything one had decided to do. . . . The process was its own reward.

Robyn Davidson

Adventure is an undertaking that implies danger or unknown risks, and that is precisely what makes it an exciting or remarkable experience. Travel just about anywhere becomes adventure when there are no strings attached—least of all, big bucks or some kind of special courage. Why? Because travel is a calling more than anything else. And when something bigger than you calls to you, grace supplies the means—be it money or gumption.

I've experienced times when the unknown risk is money, and at those times, financial risk is integral to making the trip an adventure. Isn't benevolence the principle upon which we trust and move on God's good earth? Benevolence happens when someone who believes in spite of what she doesn't see makes a leap of faith.

Is lack of daring holding you back from travel? Courage is something you take from the warehouse of love and life, not a quality handed to you on a silver platter. After all, if you're not afraid, then bravado isn't really brave. Those who have learned to sail or fly or float or simply to keep walking know the truth: heroism happens when a person is tempted by fear to hold back yet moves ahead anyway.

During the hurried middle-of-the-night exodus from Egypt, Pharaoh's Hebrew slaves embraced the adventure of their lives. Making a dash for the Red Sea—and beyond it, freedom— women carried bowls of unleavened dough on their shoulders. I wonder what they were thinking as they crossed the sea, mud squishing between their toes, watching walls of water held at bay on either side. Pharoah's strong men were hot on their tails. What were the women feeling? Crazy with fear? Yet once safe on the other side, the women brought out their timbrels to dance. Led by Miriam, their singing was a celebration of freedom on the road thousands of years before Jack Kerouac made a name for himself.

We were all born with winning tickets—and cashing them in is a simple matter of altering our cadence as we walk through the world.

Rolf Potts

Creature Comforts on the Road

Take a bit of home with you wherever you go. Here are easy-to-carry ideas for cozy evenings in a foreign place or a little bit of glamour on the road:

- **A candle** (and matches or a lighter) can kindle an evening and turn a stale hotel room into a fragrant resting place.
- **Aromatic massage oil** works wonders when rubbed on your shoulders, arms, and feet after a bath at the end of a long day.
- **Photos of your children, family, or sweetheart** can bring home to you wherever you go. Whether kept by your bedside table or in an envelope, you can pull out photos and linger over them while waiting for trains, planes, and buses.
- **A ziplock bag of your favorite healthy snack** (flavored almonds, trail mix, or dry cereal) can come to the rescue when you're hungry and there's no minimart in sight.
- **Favorite quotes copied into a tiny notebook** for your pocket or bag will jolt your faith when you feel discouraged or lonely.
- **A hot water bottle** is my favorite remedy for cold rooms or chilly climates. (They come in mini sizes too!)
- **A pair of fleece socks** gives you warm fuzzies and is the best luxury for tired feet—lightweight too.
- **Blank gift cards** for notes of appreciation left for others are a necessity. You'll always want to have some on hand for a special person you meet along the way.
- **Love letters** from your darling remind you of warm thoughts from far away when mail can't keep up with you.
- **A favorite placemat or small table decoration** brings cheer. A friend of mine remembers a blue metal bowl that always came out at dinnertime as her Jewish family traveled across Europe from Poland in the early 1940s.

Today, traveling by necessity has been replaced with luxury tours. Agencies and airline corporations have plans aplenty to fulfill your getaway dreams, along with a certain take-charge air of diplomacy and authority. But you don't necessarily need them. Such resources are fine, of course, for any who are able and willing to pay someone else to do the groundwork. Professionals can provide bountiful ideas about where to go, what to see, and where to eat. But not one of them can give you the key ingredient to any trip: the personal epiphany, the experience, the insight, the "moment" that is yours alone, the one thing you are looking for and can, in all truth, expect the trip to give you—remember Hagar?

Every place on earth holds a gift for you. Even if it's just the next city up the I-5. Even if it's the jungles of Mozambique. The gift of place is the reason you go at all, but no travel agency can guarantee you'll find that gift. Not even the best travel guide can point it out, and no amount of money can buy it. Only your relationship with yourself and with God will allow you to see clearly enough to discover it. The cost of a ticket or the amount of money you spend on lodging means far less than the intention with which you set out into the wide world.

A sprightly Old Testament character, the Shulamite, illustrates the power of this intention. We read in Song of Solomon how she shifts from the innocent and passive "Lead me away!"[1] spoken in the beginning of the song to a passionate and assertive "Come, my beloved," adding, "let us go forth to the field." This is appropriate since the word *pilgrimage* literally means "into the fields." To her companion she wonders aloud, "Let us see if the vine has budded, whether the grape blossoms are open, and the pomegranates are in bloom."[2] The Shulamite maiden isn't just sightseeing. She is looking for an epiphany reminiscent of Hagar's.

I have found over and over again that travel is something you do because you have a yearning for it, not because you have a bank account for it. Travel is what happens when you're willing to put yourself in a position where, come hell or high water, you really want to go. Self-help gurus say that whatever you focus on expands, and I have found this to be true. What you're looking for, really looking for, will come to you as if on the wings of a gilded bird. Wait and watch for the unexpected.

> To seek. Not to find, not to end but to always seek a beginning. That was what the trip had become . . . a pilgrimage only to seek.
>
> Gary Paulsen

I'd wanted to go back to Israel ever since I lived there after college. When in midlife my editorial mailbox contained a letter of invitation to visit Israel along with other journalists, I eagerly accepted. We were to be guests of the Israeli Ministry of Tourism. I even went there a second time five years later when another editor declined because she was afraid. Trips to Haiti during the U.S. embargo of that country and to religious sites in Turkey for public relations promotion came in the wake, each bearing magnificent gifts of place. Each of these trips was birthed by grace that must have sprung from my willingness to accept risk and dare to go.

I can't help thinking of African American Harriett Tubman in this context. Born a slave in 1820 and escaping at age twenty-nine, she became the Moses of her people. Throughout the Civil War, she traveled as a scout, spy, nurse, and cook in the Union army. Once she knew the ropes, she became a conductor along the Underground Railroad, a secret network of safe houses for runaway slaves on their way north.

If you want to go badly enough—anywhere—you'll find a way. After visiting Europe with my sister in 1970, what I thought would be a once-in-a-lifetime trip led to perpetual longing. I decided to find a way to get back there. The following year, my final year of college, I worked the night shift as a waitress at a pancake house every weekend (tips weren't great at that hour). I didn't buy school clothes, shoes, or makeup. I didn't go to concerts or movies. I saved every penny I earned, because I knew I had to get back to the places where I'd left my heart.

At the end of the year, I'd saved enough to buy a one-way ticket to London, a pair of leather boots (I took no other shoes), and enough to live on for a few months—if I was careful. I arranged a job in Essex, England, that offered board and room. Once there, I used my meager savings to take day trips by train one day each week, walking everywhere else, rationing my allowance for food, and never buying anything. It was a humble start, but I ended up living overseas a total of two years, working in four other countries.

The adventure was nonstop, but of course, I made many sacrifices, or what would have been sacrifices for the average tourist. I ate only what I could buy with coins: a sausage from a street vendor, bread or cheese from a grocer, a piece of fruit from the open market. I rode the railways overnight to save hotel or hostel costs, and this when traveling at night was a huge inconvenience. Before the European Common Market, the train stopped at every national border (that's often!), where police came aboard and awakened sleeping passengers to check passports. By day, I didn't see a lot of what normal tourists see because I hadn't the money for tickets to art galleries and museums. But I saw much that ordinary tourists never get to: alpine forests full of wildflowers, the intriguing faces of Palestinians waiting—sometimes for hours—for a bus, the moving image of crippled children "jumping" rope in the slums of Port au Prince.

Duct Tape: The Traveler's Friend

Pack the duct tape and you'll find a thousand uses—with no worries. It's lightweight, tears easily into the size you want, and packs conveniently because other items can be tucked inside the roll. Besides, just for fun, you can get it in all colors. Uses for go girls:

- **To rid tired traveling feet of corns** (and warts), use duct tape to adhere an ordinary aspirin to your foot. (Some folks insist the duct tape works by itself; you don't need the aspirin.)
- **Bind a ripped suitcase**, bag, or a broken zipper with tape that can be easily reapplied or replaced when reopening.
- **Close up boxes to send home extra stuff**. You can find a cardboard box free. Tape it up and send it off.
- **Repair broken shoes** that wear out when you can't get a new pair immediately or don't want to part with a favorite pair. Or mend a rip from the inside of a piece of clothing like jeans.
- **Use with cotton pads as Band-Aids** for blisters on your feet and toes. You can even use tape as a tourniquet or bandage in case of injury.
- **Get a grip on a tricky or stuck lid** on anything from nail polish to a jar of pickles.
- **Fasten things onto your backpack**. Wind it through loops or attach items to the insides of pockets so they don't fall out (this foils pickpockets too). Use twisted tape to attach things to the loops of your blue jeans if no key chain or string is available.

Travel is a voyage into that famously subjective zone, the imagination, and what the traveler brings back is an ineffable compound of himself and the place, what's really there and what's only in him.

Pico Iyer

If you want to go someplace but don't seem to be able to afford it or can't justify the money you'd be spending, volunteer for something. Work in an orphanage in Baja, California, teach English to Japanese students in Tokyo, build the walls of a church in Haiti, help deliver medical supplies to Costa Rica. Many schools or missions offer room and board for your services, and many nonprofit organizations offer grants for transportation to Third World countries. Apply for scholarships to study abroad or accompany a group of students as a chaperone for a discounted price. If you've always wanted to visit New York City, you don't have to go to the opera or a Broadway show to have fun. Skip dinner in Manhattan and sign up to serve in a downtown mission for a holiday like Thanksgiving or Christmas; you'll get a free dinner alongside heaps of satisfaction. Don't shop for souvenirs at Macy's; the treasure you'll take home will be invisible, but it will last forever.

On a semester abroad, Tirza Wibel's experience in Britain, other than the airfare, cost no more than staying in her degree program at her university. The plane ticket was absorbed into her low-interest student loans. When she returned to the States, Tirza was hired as an intern editor for *BritRail* magazine, allowing her the further adventure of living in New York City an entire summer. The job paid enough to cover all her expenses, including sightseeing on weekends.

As a middle school student, Leyah Jensen spent a week in the Dominican Republic. The trip was offered by Compassion International in return for an article to be published in a Christian kids' magazine. It was there Leyah's vision for the underprivileged and love of travel were kindled to red-hot flame. During college, she spent six weeks in an orphanage in Haiti just because she realized it was possible and, for her, necessary. Though she suffered daily hunger and often fear—or maybe because of it—Leyah's photojournalism revealed something beyond black faces and captured the soul of poverty.

Lissa Jensen decided, once all her high school credits were completed, to spend her final semester working in Mexico. While

Capturing That Moment— without a Camera

Oh, the places you'll go! The things you'll see! The things you'll do! When trying to record everything you've experienced becomes tedious, give yourself a break. Create a whimsical diary documenting just one moment in your day, your week, or your trip:

- **Focus on just a few details**. Choose one moment of the day that you wish to remember forever just the way it was. Log the date and time of day—a little ritual to prime the pump.
- **Get up close and personal** by noting the location as closely as you can pinpoint it: "I'm standing on the west ridge of the Grand Canyon, within three feet from its drop." Or "It's raining in Central Park. I'm huddled in my raincoat on a bench under a huge blossoming tree."
- **Write in present tense to describe the setting using your five senses**: exactly what you see, hear, feel (the chill of the wind or an arm around your back), smell, or taste (the air or the lemon drop you're sucking on).
- **Take a step back and describe anything in the distance**: architecture or city skyline, a forest, or bakery shelves. Look for details that take an extra eye to see.
- **Show what's happening**. Write vivid. Write simple. Are you disappointed or celebrative when you visit the Alamo? Do you find it too commercialized, or does it bring back memories of childhood fantasies— riding with Davy Crocket and Daniel Boone?
- **Write your emotions**. Blurt on paper. Be raw. Be real. Be perfectly honest. Don't hold back. Do you feel a sense of God's presence camping under the stars at Yosemite's half dome? Are you afraid or exhilarated as your parasail rises off the water over Lake Couer d'Alene?
- **Reflect on how you might interpret the moment months from now**— these are insights you may not have known you were receiving. Elicit yearnings or goals that arise in you, a sense of purpose, or questions about your moment.

classmates were agonizing over a date to the prom or what color dress they would wear, Lissa was agonizing over which dirty, hungry kid to fall in love with first. Okay, so it wasn't Puerto Vallarta or Cabo San Lucas, graduation-gift destinations that many of her friends enjoyed. But her stay was free and the payoff enormous.

Each of these girls brought home beautiful, priceless souvenirs—the kind you have no trouble getting through customs and upon which the government imposes no tax. Now that's a switch!

Avoiding danger is no safer in the long run than outright exposure. Life is either a daring adventure or nothing.

Helen Keller

Although I'm no longer as emotionally agile as I used to be, no longer so unafraid or willing to take on the world and whatever may come, I've often wondered, now with my children raised, *Where would I go if I dared? What would I do?* I am more cautious, more nervous, but would I do it all again? I read *Under the Tuscan Sun* by Frances Mayes, and I knew I wanted to live that story. Material accessories don't mean much anymore, and neither do the *trap*-pings of success. I don't punish myself, but if necessary, I can live on V-8 juice and cottage cheese. I can sleep on a wooden deck or stone terrace or sack out on the sofa. That doesn't mean I don't appreciate sleeping in a soft, silky bed; it just means that if sleeping on the floor of a ferryboat means going somewhere at the same time, and if needing to sleep in a warm bed means not going at all, I can sleep on the floor of a ferryboat.

I have a lot to learn about travel now, because things are always changing. In the 1970s I knew how to travel inexpensively; that needs to be updated: old dog, new tricks. Recently, planning a trip to my niece's wedding in San Diego, I picked a cheap hotel in an inferior location just to save money. Then my Internet-savvy daughter asked, "Why are you staying *there*, Mother? You can get the Marriott at the same cost if you go online and make a low bid at a travel website." Voilà! Within an hour I had a room at the Marriott in an upscale beach town for less than a room at the other hotel under the freeway overpass.

Of course, every individual will have personal standards for comfort and to maintain hygiene, health, and vitality. But we probably need less than we think we need. We need less than what we've become accustomed to. The old Mennonite adage "Use it up, wear it out, make it do, or do without" can be called upon as truth more times than not when traveling. In fact, sometimes, and often, it is in the making do that an emotional or spiritual epiphany comes in disguise.

The point is, do you want to go or not? Has someplace special been calling your name? Then dare to make it possible. God says it already is! Want to visit the Cinqua Terra on the Italian Riviera? By all means. Participate in a conference on Molokai? Why not? There are ways around every obstacle with prayer and patience and the attitude that everything is possible.

That is why a journey is the best preparation for life, whether the trip be around the next bend in the road or all the way to Oz. Travel reawakens sensibilities, because you must trust God and yourself. You become "curiouser and curiouser" like Alice in Wonderland. You let go of assumptions and judgments about culture and people while sharpening the skill of graceful discernment. With time and experience on the road, you convey confidence. You may not always know where you are going, but you come to know who you are—and that woman will surprise you!

Unpacking Nepal

A Pilgrim's Profile: Diana Mount

How I learned on a starry night peering
toward Mount Everest how big the world
is—and how beautiful!

Travel is more than the seeing of sights, it is a change that goes
on, deep and permanent, in the ideas of living.

Miriam Beard

The Lost Horizon, filmed in Tibet, is one of Diana Mount's favorite movies, so when the opportunity to go trekking in Nepal fell into her lap, Diana rose to the occasion. "I was forty-six and going through perimenopause," she says. "I'll be honest; I had suffered depression for years but didn't even know it. It wasn't until I got so far away from home and everything familiar that I thought, *Here are these people happy with nothing! My life is comfortable, full of beautiful things, but I don't have the beautiful feelings the women in Nepal have, and I want that.*"

44

Diana, of Sisters, Oregon, says what drove the point home was being uncomfortable and knowing she couldn't do anything about it and would just have to get through it. "I couldn't escape the discomfort," she says. "At home if I'm hungry, I go get something to eat. If I'm cold, I pull on a sweater or an extra blanket. If I'm thirsty, I have so many beverages to choose from. In Nepal, I knew I had to bear the cold and hunger without relief."

Diana's mother asked her before she left, "Isn't there an easier way to do this?"

Diana told her, "I have been given this opportunity; I can't imagine saying no to it."

On her first day, hiking alone to the place where she would meet her sherpa, a snowstorm came in and created a whiteout all around her. "I found that it was not a clear path," Diana says. "There were lots of switchbacks, and I got confused. A group of local women came up behind me and, realizing I was lost, showed me the way." When Diana reached their village, they served her cups of hot tea. One of them made a meal for her of eggs and potatoes. "I gave them each a colorful scarf," she says, "but what they gave me was far more beautiful."

The terrain in Nepal meant encountering mountains, valleys, and a little bit of everything in between. Diana and her sherpa, Lhakpa, climbed from 4410 meters upward to the highest point and her goal, 5540 meters. She was shaken by the impact of the altitude. "Some days we covered less territory but climbed straight up. The lack of oxygen made things ten times more difficult. Also, at higher altitudes the stoves were fueled by yak dung instead of wood. Pretty soon everything smelled like dung! It was an unusual experience."

Lhakpa, who carried one of her two backpacks, knew just a few words of English, but the two learned to make hand gestures. "I'm not real chatty anyway," Diana says, "and I wasn't there to make conversation."

"The hard part was always being cold," Diana admits with emotion. "We'd get to a village about 2:30 p.m., and the host families didn't start their little wood stoves until two or three hours later. We'd wait around the teahouse in a cold room. We had to wait even longer for them to cook dinner—rice and whatever vegetables could be had. We'd warm up a little, then retire to primitive bedroom chambers that were always freezing."

Showers in an outhouse-type building included warm water. "But afterward I'd be shivering," Diana adds. "The first day my teeth rattled so badly, I decided to shower only once a week." Drinking water was a key issue. Diana had heard that bottled water couldn't be trusted, so she got boiled water from her hosts, cooled it, and then filtered it into her water containers each day. "You could carry only so much because of the weight," she says. "Drinking water was premium."

On her trek, Diana thought about things she'd always wanted to do back home but hadn't accomplished because of depression. "I spent a lot of time writing in my journal, and I asked the question, *Why am I here?* many times."

Diana says that close to the top, at Gorak Shep, she started to feel sick from the altitude. "I wanted to stop, but I knew I had to keep going to Kala Patthar, our goal the next morning," she says.

At Kala Patthar we looked down on base camp for climbing Mount Everest. A lot of people were gathering there for expeditions. "I had my photograph taken there in front of the highest mountain in the world," Diana says, "then we returned to Lobuche for the night. I was exhausted. I was just out of it, so I went to bed early."

"About 2:00 in the morning I woke up," she says. "My headache had gone. I went out into the darkness. Yak bells were tinkling in the distance. The moon and stars were bright and clear. That was the moment.

"I can look back on my experience and know I met my climbing goal," Diana adds, "but that night is the one that changed things. That's when I made up my mind to get the help I need." Diana says she could have stayed at home and made the same decision, but she doesn't know that it would have been characterized by the same kind of spiritual catharsis. "It was the adventure and the time of solitude on the trip that gave me courage to try some alternatives to my depression and to do the things I'd been putting off for years," she says.

Back home now for a year, Diana adds, "I've had energy. I've been excited.

"I also watched the families in Nepal," Diana says. "I saw how spiritual and cultural traditions are entwined in their day from the moment they get up. I observed how they take care of each other at all ages, often in contrast to the American style of doing family. One of the most poignant changes for me was realizing I just want my daughter in my life, I don't need to impose my expectations on her."

"I know now that I have no choice but to live in the present moment," Diana says. "In the middle of that starry, moonlit night, I saw how big the world is—and how beautiful. Why shouldn't I be happy just to be a part of it?"

3

God's Outward Bound School

God's School for Faith

Traveler—there are no roads. Roads are made by walking.

Spanish Proverb

When my middle daughter, Leyah, discovered the time-worn flea market just blocks from her dorm room in Providence, Rhode Island, she didn't see grimy trinkets or cheesy cast-off junk for sale. She saw a fairy-tale underworld city. In the dark, cavernous hideaway of a dilapidated warehouse where down-and-outers congregated, every time-scarred, weathered face held a story. The market, a place most city dwellers wouldn't dare to venture, was for Leyah an adventure waiting to happen. Here, in a tangled maze of sloppy booths and shops selling stuff nobody wanted, she found something that moved her.

Leyah came often enough to become friends with the proprietors and vendors. She laughed at their jokes and appreciated their quirks. When she learned the city had condemned the building in order to build a complex of high-end shops, she mourned the loss. These were real people living real lives. What mattered to them was to go to work each day and find community. Soon they were to be unemployed and disconnected.

Writing their stories, Leyah painted an unexpected picture—a charming old market personified in intriguing characters, soon to be a relic nobody would remember. *Providence* magazine, a glossy monthly, picked up the story and published it for the society crowd, running whimsical photographs. The viewpoint was a kind of redemptive commemoration to a time that was and the loss of something few had valued.

Traveling through the world by observing and valuing what others don't is another way to name the-God-Who-Sees as Hagar did. We are made in God's image. The one who travels—across town or across the country—will see clearly what others don't even notice. Isn't this the heart of pilgrimage and spiritual adventure? It is to find a way beyond the not-seeing and not-feeling that dehumanizes the world.

God over me, God under me, God before me, God behind me, I on thy path, O God, Thou, O God, in my steps.

Carmina Gadelica

Mythologist Joseph Campbell claimed the best way to call out each others' humanity is through the act of "tourism." He encouraged people everywhere to "go somewhere and meet somebody else." Tourism helps us look past artificial divisions, he said. It demystifies the stranger. At its best, tourism is not about sightseeing for escapism. It is powerful because it takes us beyond our provincial and prejudiced thinking.[1] To travel is to keep an eye on what is invisible, seeing the old in new ways or the new in old things. It is to see what you see but do not know you see until you open your heart—to a culture, a people group, an individual.

50

Healthy, Cheap Eats: The Best on the Road

Grocery stores are the least expensive places for staples that serve as carry-along snacks. You will also find a good variety of things you can cook in a hostel or motel kitchen, at a campsite, or on a temporary stay with friends. Choose simple items that can be concocted without much fuss or mess: individual containers of instant soup, packets (not cans) of tuna fish, smoked or dried meats, pop-top cans of juice, and bottled water. Pack a pocket knife or collapsible scissors to open difficult packaging.

Specialized markets offer the best quality and freshest products. Although pricing is usually by weight, it works best to order by amount (four slices of cheese, for example, with two pears and six carrots). Keep in mind that many vendors abroad do not want you to pick up the produce yourself. Point to the pieces you want; be considerate of local custom.

Vegetable and fruit markets can be found in almost any country. Look for open-air vendors and farm-grown produce. Bring a small bottle of organic veggie-wash soap to clean produce in the restroom or at a drinking fountain. There are certain places in the world where you should not eat fresh produce, so first check your guidebook.

Cheese markets can be confusing, but shopping in them usually results in a delicious adventure. Try something you've never tried before but think you'll like. In some places, you may ask for a sample. Observe local customers and follow suit.

Bakeries! No one should ever be on a low-carb diet when traveling where bread can be purchased fresh and hot. Part of the adventure is picking out a small cake or pastry to devour right on the spot.

Beware of higher prices at fast food franchises overseas. Go for local flavor at neighborhood cafés or burger joints instead. Ask where the locals go—and what the specialties are. Be prepared to discover something new.

Delis let you pick up protein and package it any way you want—more of this, less of that. Try the local olives, pickles, or mustards. One of the best things typically is the friendliness of the people; often the owner is making the sandwiches and serving them too.

Pizza shops are standard, but be forewarned: Euro-style pizza is very different from American pizza. It usually comes with just sauce and cheese—not all the toppings we've come to expect. Go with the flow, though, and think of how to delight in the variety.

Adventure is not dichotomous with observation, contemplation, or reflection. Adventure is to actually live those qualities. Adventurers take a profound and personal view of nature and humanity. We take nothing at face value. We look harder and think deeper about everything. We return home and tell the stories of what we've seen, kneading them into bread for the nourishment of the world. As Phil Cousineau writes so poignantly, "We cross borders, but they are not just on the map."[2]

To see with a broad vision is your calling as a pilgrim on earth. We are all journalists of the heart. How often do you see the world and all its faults, imperfections, and foibles as if you are looking at the most precious thing ever created? Might you examine what you see as a scientist discovering a new breed of aquatic creature that breaks all the rules for what you think you know? What you are so sure of?

Jewish philosopher Martin Buber writes in *I and Thou* that "relation is reciprocity." He contrasts the "I-Thou" relationship with the "I-It" relationship where people exist as "an object among objects . . . assigned its measure and boundary."[3] This "I-It" is what Joseph Campbell warned against when he encouraged us to travel. The "I-Thou" is discovered when we see sights and strangers not as objects to be gawked at but as beings with an integrity of their own, a quality to be discovered and valued.

When you see this way, you offer something back to the culture through which you are passing. Imagine if the crusaders of the Middle Ages had been given cameras instead of swords. How might they have encountered the sights and townspeople and holy places with a different result? Traveling from England or France all the way across Turkey and into the Holy Land, would they have been as destructive—crippling and killing anything or anyone who did not look, act, or claim to be "Christian"? Had they cameras instead of swords and chain mail, would they have looked in a redemptive way as does the-God-Who-Sees?

Real travel is not a consumer item, it is a private, idiosyncratic thing, the traveler feeling the urge to go forth, unprotected, to confront the unfamiliar.

Dervla Murphy

To be a pilgrim is to tread lightly on this earth. In this country, we buy a parcel of ground, a particular lot, and fence it in. We nurture the ground within its borders, planting gardens or grass and trees. We pass on the value of the land to our children when we leave the earth, or we make money off it by selling it to someone else. Many people in our culture have made themselves wealthy with the trade of real estate. We think, because of this ability and custom, that we actually own the land.

To be a spiritual adventurer is to realize that ownership of anything on this earth is impossible. Our calling is to participate in offering life back to the world, not claiming the world for ourselves. We make eye contact with people, meet kindred and unkindred spirits, find and create community with people like and unlike ourselves. We are to engage in this with intention and generosity. Touching the earth, we let the earth touch us back. In the act of pilgrimage, we engage in an affectionate relationship with culture wherever we live and wherever we go.

A person who is alive is constantly getting lost. The big thing . . . is to realize that this is your own adventure, and that all the field guides . . . holding up mirrors can only flash you . . . a glimpse of your own story. It's yours to savor. It belongs to no one else.

Bonnie F.

Inspirational Reading for the Road

A New Testament
Simplicity by Richard Rohr
West with the Night by Beryl Markham
The Way of the Traveler by Joseph Dispenza
Women into the Unknown by Marion Tinling
Passionate Quests by Sonia Melchett
Out of Africa by Isak Dinesen
Beyond the Looking Glass (Alice in Wonderland) by Lewis Carroll
Pilgrim at Tinkers Creek by Annie Dillard

When I was a little girl in the 1950s, I liked taking walks with my father. In the days before television, or at least before my family had a television, we used to walk around the block or through the downtown area of our small Kansas town, traversing its red brick streets after dinner in the evenings. When my short legs grew weary from keeping up with his longer ones, we'd head back. My dad would almost always recite the story of Christopher Columbus. He'd tell how Columbus's crew of sailors grew weary, sick, anxious, rebellious. The food rotted. The ship appeared to be lost at sea. There was no shore in sight day after mindless day.

"Turn back," the crew finally demanded. "Turn back," they insisted day after day. But Columbus's answer was always the same: "Sail on. Sail on. Sail on and on. Sail on and on and on." Through repetition of these words, my father made certain I got the lesson. When life got stormy in years to come, I would remember those words. In living accordingly, I have often been surprised and delighted by what lay waiting to be discovered farther on.

The legacy of Christopher Columbus remains a part of my spiritual heritage. The lure of the unknown is a beacon. To sail on and on has become part of my life's modus operandi. Once I had my own little girls, my father sometimes invited them, one at a time, to accompany him on his predawn walks. The girls' tingly excitement at being awakened in the darkness to walk with Papa was felt throughout the house. But the trek to the donut store usually turned to discouragement once they realized how very far it was. When their small feet had pounded too many yards of sidewalk, down a steep hill, around the bend, and along a street that seemed to stretch on forever, their grandpa would start the story of Christopher Columbus.

"Sail on," Papa would tell them. "Sail on," he shouted as light found its way onto the horizon from the east. "Sail on. Sail on. Sail on and on." Of course, my father knew that the donut shop was just around the corner. Before long, the bright orange and white sign would appear, and the reward confirmed the lesson of Columbus, engraving it on their hearts as it had been engraved on mine. The legacy he left them: providence rewards those who move ahead and move on.

To venture causes anxiety, but not to venture is to lose one's self.

Søren Kierkegaard

To launch your ship into deep waters takes confidence in your own abilities to manage whatever comes and trust in a God who has promised to provide along the way. What may seem to hold the potential of disaster will turn most decidedly into the discovery of something you would have never expected: a whole new world. Bring to your trip an eagerness to find that for which you may have been tempted to just wait until heaven to find.

55

The magic of travel is that you create your own experience along the open road. Play more. Risk more. Interact with what you see and the people you meet. In another culture, it is always an ice breaker to ask about people's children; inquire about their names, their pets, their jobs. Watch for what makes their eyes light up and follow the thread of that conversation. Find a way to become a part of the scene in more than just a photo op.

Engage in the affection of pilgrimage. Every trip brings us around full circle, away from fear to compassion. Every trip disentangles us from our own insecurities. It takes us way beyond what we think we can do. I suppose I got my first taste of travel when my family made a trip to Victoria, British Columbia, and Yellowstone National Park when I was six years old. About all I remember is the wild frenzy of flowers at the Butchart Gardens and wading through snow in sandals to feed the chipmunks in Wyoming. But the trip changed me.

Later, in my high school years, church caravans to Mexico gave me a taste of real pilgrimage. Strangely enough, what made an impression on me was not the poverty of the people with whom we played and ate and worshiped. It was the poverty of the missionary who lived with his wife in a small mobile home in a dusty village. They had no plumbing, no stores, no schools for their children. They lived and served. That's all. Their devotion to the land, the people, and their calling has never left me. This man and woman lived as true pilgrims on earth.

Since that time, I've been through the swankiest areas of Europe and seen its most fabulous art and beauty: Notre Dame in Paris, the Sistine Chapel in Rome, Chagal's windows at the Hadassah University Hospital Synagogue in Israel, Rembrandt's haunting paintings in Amsterdam. As one who owned nothing but a small backpack with a plastic coffee cup swinging from it, I have been rich. Yet always, in all places, the dusty Mexican

Nowhere or Everywhere?
A Story from Mexico

I think about my trip. I think about the little boy who saw my empty lap and took it without a word. I think about his sleep there, and my knees, collapsed and prickled with numbness under the weight that had fallen on them. And I think about how, despite my legs, I wanted him to sleep forever.

In Mexico I was scared. I was lost. I did not feel at home. I got a cold, felt self-conscious and sometimes harassed. I left my face plain. I felt hunger. I cried. I watched a little girl feed a baby from coffee cream packets on the side of a dirt road. I slept alone in a dark room with five babies dependent on me. Never before, with my food and my friends and my comforts, have I ever felt alive like I did then. Why do I long for those old feelings? Because inside of them, I am suddenly, terrifically, unspeakably, humbly yet so proudly, tangibly, grotesquely, laughingly, crazily, mortally, dumbly alive.

Today, at home again, I can't help but feel I've gone nowhere. Everything moves in fast forward and in jolted separations of space. I watch myself from a distance, with my fifty-dollar shoes and my strawberry waffles (the ones I threw out this morning). I am worried. I am guilty. Above my bed, the wall is cluttered with pictures of nameless faces—faces I touched with my own two hands: pictures of happy children who clung to me at one point in time, pictures of people whom I loved until it was a cross I bore, until it hurt to love them so much.

Joy Melissa Jensen

village and the missionary who lived there have weighted my soul like ballast on a ship.

> The moment you've made up your mind to go somewhere, do something you want, the most difficult part of the trip is behind you.
>
> Rob Sangster

I once heard a doctor tell his wife on their way home from a visit to impoverished Christians in Romania, "Honey, we're never going to have money." And when I see, really see, with that sort of perspective, money is not even a question. I realize that adventure coming full circle to compassion makes one far wealthier than material things can. Spiritual adventure is its own reward, and some people think money can buy it, but that is a deception.

Adventure can be had every day just by being open, letting your desires be known, offering them up to a benevolent universe, and enrolling in God's Outward Bound school. Adventure is a way of life you can live every day. I think of Joan of Arc, a waif in the overbearing presence of the men with whose lives she became involved. In tattered jacket and pants, she has become a myth more than a real person and her life little more than a mini epic.

In a brilliant 1928 silent film, *The Passion of Joan of Arc*, directed by Carl Theodor Dreyer and featuring Renee Falconetti, Joan is no longer the brave heroine who led the French army to victory. She is a vulnerable nineteen-year-old girl, frightened, humiliated, and distanced from the saints of the ages. In one small sequence, she is led into a small, dark chamber and left alone to sob. The camera switches to a simple patch of light on the floor where windowpanes diffuse light in the shape of a cross.

Stories of women adventurers make us realize that faith is possible even in the very center of uncertainty and doubt. Our stories are not about religion or female martyrdom or playing out some heroic destiny. As one film expert said, the story of Joan of Arc is stripped down: it is about a pair of eyes. Is God there? Spiritual adventure is about the strange ways bridges are built between God and humanity. Each one of us—even when our travels leave us questioning—is building a way for the world to embrace the-God-Who-Sees.

Part 2

Explore the World;
Discover Yourself

4

Mapping Your Terrain

From the Inside Out

I only went out for a walk, and finally concluded to stay until
sundown. Going out, I found out I was really going in.

John Muir

It's called "life mapping" to go back and trace the route you've
come from, build altars at your intersections with faith, and place
crosses or *descansos* to commemorate places where loss occurred.
When you work with life mapping, you identify your gifts and
dreams and plot a route to the places you want to go next. You
survey the optional paths and decide which ones you'll take.
Life mapping is about living your life with generous attention
to detail and a great deal of purpose.

I've found myself studying maps of places I'd like to go: the
new republics that used to be beyond the Iron Curtain, the Scottish Leys of Marlee, the islands off the coast of Spain. I relish

Document Your Interior Journey

Keep a small journal just for preserving your feelings and spiritual insights while traveling. Your mini journal is not a place to document where you went or what you did. It's purely about things that may have an effect on you and leave you changed. The least things—a butterfly landing near you, an accident you witnessed, classical music you heard at a concert—are all pieces of the whole. You'll be able to glance through the journal later and recall things you would otherwise have long since forgotten. Jot down:

- **Music** you heard that moved you to particular feelings.
- **Art** that inspired you and why or how.
- **People** who impressed you and why. Include what they looked like.
- **Nature or scenery** that surprised or impressed you.
- **Incidents** that frightened or shocked you.
- **Local customs or events** that gave you food for thought.
- **Sights or ideas** that raised your consciousness.
- **Words spoken or read** that brought you closer to God.
- **Serendipitous moments** with spiritual significance.
- **Anything** that lifted your soul, made you think more deeply, or made you feel something you've never felt before.

Let your documentation lead you to muse over an event, idea, or thought. Follow the trail in your mind or emotions. Wonder about it and detail honest reactions. These kinds of observations offer something—the power of being in the moment—that you can never reclaim later.

pilgrimages that follow tracks also. What would it be like to visit the old Spanish missions along the California coast and pray in each one? To follow the Santa Fe Trail looping through Kansas, my home state? Or to hike the long pathway through the English lake district?

I am intrigued by maps and by life mapping, yet I enjoy the serendipity of unexpected turns as well. "Not all who wander are lost," wrote J. R. R. Tolkien in *The Fellowship of the Ring*.[1] Life is often what happens to you while you're making other plans, isn't it? The thing is, if you're not making some kind of plans, there's no structure from which to diverge, wander off the map into somebody else's backyard, and possibly make a friend or pick a flower.

It's easy to be brave from a safe distance.

Aesop

When I was in college in Santa Barbara, California, the naughty thing to do at my small private college, unlike the beer parties on campus at the local university, was to go "estate hopping." Since our campus lay in the foothills above the city and was surrounded by huge, heavily wooded estates, there was a huge choice of adventure. The grounds of many of our neighbors were surrounded by walls of stone or brick, low enough that it was easy to hoist one another up and over them. Behind the walls lay small pieces of paradise, often not immaculately kept but green and lush from the ocean mists and fog. Old arbors, bird baths, fish ponds, trails, tea pavilions, rose gardens, or terraced orchards created Renaissance ambience for exploring. The large, villa-looking homes, old and stately with pompous windows and grand doors, were usually without sight of the gardens through which we romped.

Exploits like this were definitely "off the map" for a good little Christian girl raised to stay within precise boundaries. I was taught to stay in my own backyard and to not trespass in others', just as I was taught to color within the lines of the coloring books I loved—with pictures of characters from Disney's Snow White to sexy Natalie Wood. But somewhere between my eighteenth and fiftieth birthdays, I discovered that outside self-imposed boundaries is where the booty is.

Leif Eriksson discovered the continent of North America by being blown off course on his way to the continent he named Greenland. Columbus rediscovered North America by heading west thinking he would come more quickly to India. Both sailed outside the known boundaries of the world and, well, look what happened. Maps are good things, because they put us on a course. They point us on our way somewhere. But they are not the know all and end all.

Robyn Davidson writes about maps in her book about trekking across Australia's outback: "Whoever those people are who fly in planes and make maps of the area, they need glasses; or perhaps were drunk at the time; or perhaps just felt like breaking free of departmental rulings and added a few little bits and pieces of imaginative topography, or even, in some cases, rubbed out a few features in a fit of solitary anarchic vice."[2]

Even with a really good map, we'll be rerouted on detours, be delayed by unexpected roadblocks, and face perplexing crossroads. When you set out on a trip, study your map, but be prepared to be guided by your spirit as well. After all, pilgrimage is about Adventure (notice the capital *A*?). In life, as on a trip, we will eventually stumble over some terrain that is not like it is supposed to be. We will be thrown into a quandary where our survival may depend on a map—or not. On a trip, we may have a guide who knows the place inside and out, every pothole and every turn. In life, however, there are few guides, and they, if they are wise, will be like the ancient wizard Merlin: not available just when we need them most.

Like God with the Israelites, good guides will hide themselves when it's necessary. The prophet Isaiah exclaimed, "Truly You are God, who hide Yourself."[3] Have you ever experienced this God who likes to play hide-and-seek? I have many a time. I wonder why God wraps himself in a mystique of darkness or a disguise, waiting to see what I will do first.

God does not answer every question I ask. He often answers my questions with another question. Sometimes, like with Job, God seems entirely disinterested in the questions. He knows something we don't know. I suppose British parliamentarian General Oliver Cromwell knew something of God's wisdom and the beauty of bewilderment when he said, "Man never rises so high as when he knows not whither he is going."[4] That goes for women too, of course.

The landscape is shaped by the consciousness of the person who crosses it.

Holly Morris

I have to admit, there are times when I hate maps. I want to have my eyes open to the world around me, not down on a piece of paper someone has drawn. Often, I prefer to intuit my way forward or just ask for directions. During my first stay in Israel, I decided one evening to travel by bus to Tel Aviv to visit a family I'd met at church. I found their apartment, but since they weren't at home, I decided to walk to the beach before catching the bus back to the farm where I lived on the Plain of Sharon. The beach was beautiful at sunset. I walked and walked. But when I headed back I got lost. Darkness fell. I had no idea where I was or how to get back to the city.

I haven't a clue how I finally found my way; I remember only that I had to walk through a construction zone and past a trailer filled with men drinking and laughing. I hoped they wouldn't see me. I hoped nothing bad would happen. I was scared, but I had no other option. Certainly, traveling off the map, I was afraid. Then I remembered something: the Bible says Jesus might have called ten thousand angels to rescue him, and I knew that was true for me as well. I called on those angels! On I walked with the best air of confidence I could muster and *very* long strides. I learned that losing your way, or not being able to find it on the map, is sometimes not a big tragedy. That's how you "get" the larger lessons.

A trip is an occasion to plot the map both within and without. Where are you going? What are you likely to see besides sights listed in a brochure or on a web page? Why are you going there? What do you think you might learn from that particular place? How might you open yourself to learning and growing through your misadventures?

Adventure is worthwhile in itself.

Amelia Earhart

When I went sea kayaking in the San Juan Islands near Canada's Pacific border, it wasn't because I wanted a sunny vacation or some leisure. It was a stab at being bold and plucky. But I didn't want to go alone. I told my then fifteen-year-old daughter Lissa she was going with me and that was that. No questions asked. She didn't want to go, but she submitted for the sake of dear old Mom. I paid a fortune (okay, call it a credit card splurge) to join a

Dream Stuff for Travelers

Listen to the voices around you. Let your heart lead the way when dreaming of or planning a trip; let your gut lead the way once you begin. Incorporate all the voices you've listened to; they will not all agree, of course, but they will give you a kaleidoscopic view of where you are going or how to get there. Truth, after all, has different sides, like an accident at an intersection. If it's seen by four people, one on each corner, the truth of what happened may look amazingly different to each person, even contradictory. But when the whole picture is pieced together, the whole truth is evident. It's up to you to do the piecing when different perspectives are given on a certain place. So when dreaming of a trip but unsure where you want to go . . .

- **Evaluate your desires.** Go back to what influenced you as a child.
- **Clarify what you hope for.** Identify the best and the worst that could happen.
- **Create a tentative time plan** that suits your style, pocketbook, and schedule.
- **Think about how to pace yourself**—fast and furious, deliberate and steady, or slow and wandering. What's your style?
- **Build an itinerary** for a tentative destination.
- **Emotionally connect** with your plan. Imagine yourself there. What are you wearing? What are you eating? Who are you with? Put up photos of that place, cut out newspaper clippings, or collect quotes about it for inspiration. Journal your feelings about this place.
- **Examine anything that may hold you back.** Reexamine your perceived limitations. Does it make you feel overwhelmed, or does it make you feel energized and excited?
- **List what you'll need for the trip.** Research the climate, mode of transport, events, recreation, and sightseeing destinations. Be sure to include supplies for your chosen type of documentation: film, sketch pad, journal, etc.
- **Consider what problems could arise.** What will you do to transcend each one? Give this some thought ahead of time. Problems are what make the trip interesting.
- **Question others.** Trust in your own capabilities.

small group tour with a guide. I wanted to do something totally out of my comfort zone but safe and with companionship. The guide would map the journey, and later I realized my interior journey was taking a parallel course.

When we arrived for the trip, we were relieved to find other single women waiting. But to our dismay, when we were divided into groups, my daughter and I ended up with only couples. In fact, she and I were to be the only kayak without a strong-armed male. This fact was later immobilizing when we realized how hard it is to paddle through rough tides. Besides, our kayak had been loaded with all the iron containers of water for the entire week.

The first day out, crossing the longest distance on the trip, the kayak manned by my daughter and me strayed off course. We started drifting. Lissa and I pulled on the oars as hard as we could, but we were no match for the swirling current. We paddled and pulled until I thought my back muscles were a bunch of mushy spaghetti. My arms ached. My face and throat were parched. Worst, I felt ashamed. We watched each of the other kayaks reach a distant shore while ours drifted mercilessly toward the open sea. I was glad my daughter had taken the front perch so she couldn't see that I started crying.

When the others had paddled to safety, I saw the guide turn around and head back toward us. At first I felt relief. He crossed the current as if it were a harmless stream, harnessed our kayak to his, and dragged us back to the group. The others stared at us with pity. No one said anything. I felt humiliated. Later I overheard the intern guide make a patronizing remark about us, adding insult to injury. The lead guide deflected it and took the blame, saying he would repack our kayak with lighter gear.

Our trip had started badly.

At the time, I didn't consider that bad start a spiritual experience. I looked to the sightings of bald eagles, the appearance

No-Cost Souvenirs

You can bring home these travel mementos without paying a cent—and to treasure a lifetime:

Stones, pebbles, rocks. Look for unusual shapes typical of local terrain: smooth pebbles from a stream, volcanic mountain rock, pockmarked beach stones. Use them as paperweights, for color at the bottom of a fish bowl, or as centerpieces on a side table. Write the name of the place from which you saved the stone or inscribe on it words to live by.

Pressed flowers, leaves, or grass. Laminate foliage for bookmarks or placemats to give as gifts, paste them into a scrapbook of your trip, arrange them as illustrations in a journal, or put them behind glass in a frame to look at every day.

Seashells. I scooped up handfuls of tiny shells off the coast at Tel Aviv and looped them into necklaces. I've picked shells one by precious one from the Oregon coast. Once, finding a pool of broken shells on a rainy beach, I pulled off my shoes and walked barefoot into the water. I wanted to feel the broken pieces jab against my feet, like a metaphor of my then broken heart. Then I saw one large, whole, pure white shell that had not been crushed by the pounding surf. I kept it as a gift of grace, reminding me where I've been and who I am.

Driftwood. Along a lake, river, or ocean or even in the high mountains where glacial snows carve and bleach broken branches, driftwood is design—God's art. It invites us to contemplate the passage of time and how life's buffeting sculpts our souls beautifully. Use it as an objet d'art in your garden.

Sand and water. Whether from the Jordan River in Galilee or Omaha Beach in Normandy, sand and water are holy things. Collect samples in a small vial that you label and date. Such natural elements from a place of pilgrimage serve as sweet reminders of our faith: pain is redemptive, life is good, freedom is precious.

Feathers. Native Americans hallowed these as decorations signifying profound meanings. Feathers remind me to take myself lightly and that there are angels all around me. Sometimes they come to you, landing at your feet. Other times they fly past; you must run to catch them. Tie them together with ribbon and beads or press them in your journal.

Tickets, maps, brochure art. Found by the pound at tourist centers, these things document what you experienced and prove you were there. Be selective. Keep in a scrapbook collage, along with your own snapshots, what tells and shows the things you loved.

of playful seals, and the spinning of black dolphins beside our vessels to accomplish that. One evening at dusk, sitting in the door of our tent on an uninhabited island, I spied far below, off the bluff, hundreds of sea lions playing in the light of a nearly full moon. Two nights later, on the Fourth of July, we watched from a high cliff as the sun sank in brilliant colors over the Pacific, the fireworks of a lifetime. But today, separated by years from that trip, what stays with me as truly spiritual are the feelings of being swept away in the current, helpless and humiliated. That relatively short escapade—blown off the map, needing to be rescued—brought me face-to-face with my own vulnerability.

I think it is important, after all, to own these feelings in a life where currents and crosscurrents intermingle and leave a person at risk. I see this in the lives of women at the state penitentiary where I volunteer. These women either are without families or pray things like this: "Lord, help my mother stop doing drugs," or "Lord, help my son over in the men's prison." Misdirected and abused growing up, most of the incarcerated women are sincere, but many find that upon release they haven't the skills to stay on the map. They haven't the strength to reach the shore. They drift in the rough current, coming face-to-face with their own vulnerability and shame. They need a guide who will turn back, compassionately harness them, and make them safe.

A traveler without observation is like a bird without wings.

Moslih Eddin Saadi

Maps fascinate me, because life pilgrimages, adventures of the mind or heart, are a lot like following maps. Get the right map, mark out your route, establish what you want to see and do.

History books, biographies, and novels will add to the mystique when you go off in search of who you are.

Do you want to find out what you love to do, what you're born to create or accomplish, what your bliss is?

Are you looking to strengthen your soul through a difficult time or a special loss?

Do you want to create a more sacred connection between you and someone else or between you and God?

Are you taking a trip and want to find out what you have to say to yourself along the way?

Are you ready to get away, observe things differently, and see yourself in a new setting?

Create in your mind a scenario of experience, but then put it away. Stuff it into your pocket. Because no matter how you plot and plan, life's winds of adversity or your innocent mistakes will at times blow you off course. When you make interior or exterior journeys, there will be times when you don't know where you're going. But like Cromwell said, and as God knows, you'll never rise so high. The Guide may step in if necessary. Or he may know better and hide himself until you discover your own reserves of strength. Whatever you do, keep paddling.

Unpacking the USA

A Pilgrim's Profile: Peggy Senger Parsons

How I learned to respect—and honor—
the lure of the open road

There is a certain relief in change, even though it be from bad to
worse! As I have often found in traveling in a stagecoach, that is
a comfort to shift one's position and be bruised in a new place.

Washington Irving

E *xtreme unction*: that's what Peggy Senger Parsons calls her
solo motorcycle trip from her home in Salem, Oregon,
to San Antonio, Texas. *Extreme*, meaning her trip exceeded the
ordinary, usual, or expected. *Unction*, meaning it was used for
spiritual anointing. "Christ can see down all roads," Peggy says.
"He doesn't abandon us when we pick a less promising one. I
believe that it is his will to travel with us, nothing else."

When invited to speak at a national Holiness Women's Clergy
conference in the spring of 1998, Peggy's reaction was mixed:

Me and six hundred Holiness women? Not in this lifetime! Then she thought, *San Antonio? I think I've just been offered a five-thousand-mile tax-deductible motorcycle ride!*

Peggy, who is a Quaker minister and licensed counselor, embarked on geographical research. She checked and rechecked maps, then projected weather conditions through every state between Oregon and Texas. As she calculated, she figured that if things went well, there'd be a side trip to the Grand Canyon.

The trip plan required Peggy to be able to ride five consecutive five-hundred-mile days. That's at least seven hours riding, ten with breaks. "My ride was a 1993 Kawasaki Vulcan," she says. "'Rosie,' for short, a faithful steed on many trips both ministerial and pleasure." Prior to the trip, Peggy sent Rosie for a thorough checkup, though the bike was in mint condition. She arranged for road service and got a cell phone. She started to lift weights and shopped for the largest strap-on bike bag she could find.

On the day of departure, weather reports showed it was snowing in every state in the west. Still, Peggy took off singing. As she passed the California-Oregon border, snow lined the highway. Sun fell behind the mountains as she passed a second mountain range that day.

"On the road I'd often be asked if I was traveling alone," Peggy says. "My custom was to reply, 'No, I'm riding with angels.' Then when people looked nervous, I'd have to add, 'No, not *those* angels, the other ones, the good guys!' I guess I should have worried when the plastic St. Michael I had securely glued to my dashboard tried to crawl off precisely at the Nevada state line. I stopped, got out my five-minute epoxy, and glued him right back on."

"There is a whole lot of nothing on route 95 through Nevada," Peggy says. "The scenery is remarkable if you like stark and barren." The longest stretch was about 120 miles of serious nothing. Toward late afternoon, Rosie choked for the second time that day. "I got out my cell phone," Peggy quickly adds.

"That's when I learned a fundamental lesson about cell phones. They need a cell tower."

The detailed story of Peggy's trip is characterized by exhaustion, spooky people, and disorientation. Angels aplenty there were also. "I was very grateful that God is better at inserting himself into our works than we are at inserting ourselves into his," she says.

By the morning of the fourth day, "the idea of adventure was wearing a bit thin," Peggy admits. She began to meditate on the words of the prophet Isaiah: "Make straight the highway . . . the valley shall be exalted, the crooked made straight, the rough places plain." Peggy adds, "I did make a few curves straight, it's hard to use only one lane when you are singing Handel with a full orchestra." By the end of the day, crossing the "real desert" in ninety-eight-degree sun, Peggy found herself haggard and "without starch." She collapsed into dreamless sleep.

The next day with seven hundred miles behind her, Peggy almost started to relax. She tensed again when Rosie began to cough and sputter. She pulled into a funky gas station and found herself in the company of a San Francisco blues band who offered to stow Rosie in their van and give her a ride all the way to San Antonio, where they had an engagement. "I wasn't afraid," Peggy says, "but what tipped the scales in favor of Rosie was my sense of honor, or perhaps foolish pride. I had said I would ride to Texas, and ride I would."

Heading toward El Paso, Peggy looked down and saw a stream of gasoline spurting like an artery onto her left leg. The vibration of the engine over time had allowed the carburetor to neatly saw through the fuel line. "I sat down on the bank of the road and let myself have a good cry," she says.

By the fifth day, Peggy's exhaustion and boredom bordering on delirium, she made San Antonio just about dark. "At the meetings that week, I experienced an odd reaction," Peggy says. "Here, the preaching was phenomenal, but I was like the Lone Ranger without Tonto. Stuck in downtown Dodge with the townsfolk. I realized I'd felt less lonely, out on the road all by myself."

Peggy presented her workshop on the prevention of family violence and began to make ready for the return trip. "The morning I left, a light rain began to fall. I literally slipped out of town," she says. "Off-again, on-again problems with the fuel line and missing more than one freak thunderstorm characterized my trip back. But at one point my heart caught up with my body and turned the corner toward home. It is always a risky thing to fly faster than your heart, but sometimes a body just can't help it."

After passing through Four Corners, New Mexico, Colorado, and Utah, where "the sky is a color I have only seen in a box of crayons," Peggy says, "the rest was a complete blur until I rolled into my driveway just in time for supper." Peggy was fifteen pounds lighter, sunburned in some places and deathly pale in others, and encrusted in dead insects. "But my place at the table was set. The people around the table had become suddenly beautiful, smart, and kind. I experienced a feeling of deep congruence. Things that I had believed before, I now knew. I would never again entertain a doubt about God's goodness.

"In some ways I felt like Dorothy," Peggy remembers. "I knew that if I ever were to go looking for adventure again, I wouldn't look farther than my own backyard." Peggy pauses, then abruptly adds, "This sentiment lasted several months. Then I started thinking about the Alaska-Canada highway!"

5

Condition the Soles of Your Soul

Exercise Gumption and Grace

> I will go before you
> And make the crooked places straight . . .
> I will give you the treasures of darkness
> And hidden riches of secret places.
>
> Isaiah 45:2–3

An *adventurer* is one who goes out in the spirit of a risk taker, disposed to seek the new and unknown. The word implies a jaunty eagerness for perilous, or at least daring, exploits. But adventure need not involve reckless foolhardiness. And of course, to do adventure is much broader than geographic movement forward. The venturing may be spiritual, emotional, or intellectual. The best thing about geographic adventure is that it usually incorporates these levels as well.

I believe the greatest adventure is to be present wherever you find yourself. The art at the heart of adventure is understanding that both danger and the ability to achieve something remarkable lie not outside of you but within. I have been enough places and met enough travelers and explorers to know that you already are, and I already am, the adventure.

What is clearly characteristic of people who travel well is the fact that adventure is more a way of seeing than it is an active undertaking. In his wonderful little book *Wherever You Go There You Are*, Jon Kabat-Zinn calls this quality—the disposition to seek the new and unknown—"heartfulness." He writes, "Perhaps the most 'spiritual' thing any of us can do is simply to look through our own eyes."[1] And, I dare say, that is the most adventurous thing we can do.

The British poet Elizabeth Barrett Browning was an invalid who never ventured much beyond her home, but she wrote what she saw in the pilgrimage that was her life: that every common bush is "afire with God."[2] Did she see less than the quintessential travel writer Pico Iyer, who has written about some of the most remote places on earth? He saw Bhutan as no one had before or has since: "There before us, at our feet, was a fairyland of light. We descended into the valley and drove past rows of many-windowed towers, as if into the heart of some enormous Christmas cake."[3]

Even the simplest pilgrim will see with the heart, like Browning and Iyer. Listen, for example, to what Kelly Winters writes of a walk in nature: "There are so many flowers, it looks like the woods are going to a wedding."[4]

I have come to learn that even extraordinary experiences are unnecessary. . . . No, on the best days, just the walking will do. . . . It also has the virtue of taking time, and over time what becomes clear is that the way is the end in itself. . . . It is only in the walking that we realize there is nowhere to go.

Roger Housden

Ten Ways to Tell of Your Travels

Finding an angle for your travel stories is like Michelangelo looking for the figure in a hulk of stone. Chip away at everything that is not the angel. Your travel story will grow out of your experience, but here are some hooks to think about:

- **Your memoir**. What's been your first-person experience of a place, culture, or person?
- **The how-to**. What would you tell others to visit or do in a particular place? How to get around or where to eat and stay? Why is it a must-see? How do you meet the local people?
- **The amusing anecdote**. Usually humorous, these quick, short pieces help listeners and readers identify with you in a personal way. Others will relate to that certain waiter in New York City, to the cab driver you met in San Francisco, or to you as the unwilling recipient of cat calls and pinches in Naples, Italy.
- **Interviews**. You might sit down with a notable geological expert, chef, entrepreneur, celebrity, or artist in the area—or even an ordinary citizen—to uncover the newsworthy drama of life.
- **Human interest stories** for newspapers or magazines will show off a place while telling about a particular aspect of culture there. Examples: courtship and marriage customs, community politics, religious celebrations, child rearing practices.
- **Special interest tales** for niche magazines. Narrow your viewpoint and focus on golfing, adventure sports, parenting, senior citizens' issues, camping, fashion, motorcycles. Angle each story for the publication's/reader's needs; be as specific as possible.
- **Meditations**. Observation and reflection of a place from your personal viewpoint will capture a sense of its personality and offer an inspirational takeaway.
- **Destination articles**. Show why a particular place has potential as a vacation trip. Who might it interest and why?
- **The feature**. Think of a particular "peg" you'll hang a travel story on for specific interests—New York City's oldest museums or the best places to kiss in the Northwest? Explore all the historical sites of a particular city, overview the architecture, or compare the local businesses.
- **News**. Report on events from Palestine. Offer bystanders a post-9/11 view of New York City or a crime victim's view of community service sentences. Look for political angles or simply the odd and unusual.

Adventure may take you roaring down an exotic river, crashing through white water insistent on claiming your life, as Tracy Johnson experienced in her midlife escapade shooting the Boh, the wildest river in Borneo. On the other hand, it may require that you gather all your inner resources just to make it through another day at a job you hate or the searing edge of betrayal by someone you love.

Adventure always requires something of you. It will demand nothing less than that you pick up your gumption and keep going, even if you have to crawl, trudge, or pull yourself along at times. Patty Danks found this when she decided to walk the Camino Santiago de Compostela over the foothills of the Pyrenees mountains. Her trek was to celebrate her sixtieth birthday and fifth year as a breast cancer survivor (see the profile of a pilgrim on page 90).

From the far north, Barbara Sjoholm tells us, "My knees shook. My stomach lurched. The uneasiness that came over me at my first sight of the Faeroe Islands, pin points of unnecessary punctuation in a vast uncaring sea, would creep up on me again and again during my time there. . . . But I knew it was only when you let go that the best things happened. That was why I traveled, and why I found it so hard sometimes."[5]

To travel is better than to arrive.

Robert Pirsig

Adventure is complex, intense, and wonderfully involving. In fact, one of its best-kept secrets is that when on an adventure, it's not necessary to have a happy ending. Jim Lovell, pilot of *Apollo 13*, never fulfilled his mission of landing on the moon, but he did succeed in bringing a shard of a spaceship home. My friend Mary still laughs over the crazy exploits of fishing and swimming in one of the globe's most exotic locations, but she returned home from a trip to Belize with a permanent "bug" lodged in her intestines. Susan sailed away from Venice with a broken heart over a romance she'd gone there to kindle. Yet the memories of kisses in slow-moving gondolas and under historic architecture will always be hers. Risks? Of course. They are inherent whenever you move through space to a place you've never gone before.

We no longer hear the voices of some of the greatest adventurers, those who exhibited a most robust heartfulness and died in the process. But I'm willing to wager that some of them would tell us the joy was worth the risk. We're all going to leave this earth at some point anyway. I like the spirit in the closing lines of *Alive*, a movie recounting the unwilling adventure of sixteen survivors who, after their plane crashed in 1972, found themselves stranded in the mountains of Chile for more than seventy days. Two of them dared to attempt crossing the mountains for help, knowing their chances were slim. "Yes, we may die," one of them told the other, "but if I die, it's going to be walking out of here."[6]

Amelia Earhart disappeared when the aircraft she was piloting solo disappeared somewhere over the South Pacific in 1937. Yet the adventurous attitude she exemplified as the first woman to pilot a plane across the Atlantic is still maintained. Christa McAuliffe, who lost her life in the 1986 *Challenger* explosion, was not a professional in the space program. But as a schoolteacher, she wanted to pass along to students what she could never teach in the classroom: courage, love of learning, and the spirit of exploration.

Adventure upsets the applecart, blows our paradigms, rattles our finest defenses. When you undertake a pilgrimage in the high spirit of a risk taker, you're exercising your option for robust change. World traveler Terry Tempest Williams has written

Celebrity of Pilgrimage

Pilgrimages of the Middle Ages were known classically as journeys to a particular place in order to worship at that place or ask for divine intervention. Relics claimed from holy sites—a shred of bone from a saint or a vial of water from a fountain—were believed to heal sickness or remove the taint of sin. Considered a "curious privilege," pilgrimage carried the implication of a purifying act.

Christians banked on the hardship involved in pilgrimage to hasten the growth of character. In some cases, pilgrimage was ordered as punishment for certain crimes. Treks were to be made in bare feet and uncomfortable clothing and involved frequent fasting. Hunger and fatigue were constant companions. St. Jerome and St. Gregory declared pilgrimage a necessity for holy living.

Later, the emphasis of pilgrimage shifted from a voluntary form of devotion to the notion of "celebrity of place." Tours were organized to places where martyrs had died or where a dramatic spiritual event happened. With the explorations of Emperor Constantine's mother, Helena, pilgrimage was elevated to an art form. Undertaken mostly by the wealthy and influential, sacred journeys brought the pilgrim prestige.

The phenomenon of celebrity motivated the middle and lower classes during the Renaissance, just as it does today. For Chaucer's pilgrims, public show, like bagpipes or bells on horses, made pilgrimage into spectacle. Pilgrims acted like tourists—embarking not prayerfully but flamboyantly. Pilgrimage turned into sightseeing. Piety became merely a camouflage for vanity. Scandals arose as outlaws and even religious authorities preyed on the sincerity of pilgrims. For would-be pilgrims who could not travel, almsgiving was solicited for those who could as a way of vicarious participation. This practice is continued today as people donate to charitable causes promoted by movie stars. The Hollywoodization of travel had begun, while St. Augustine warned that it is not by journeying but by loving that we draw nigh unto God.

Finally, pilgrimage was legislated by the church: no one was to make more than one trip beyond the seas in his lifetime. The first "holy days" or annual vacations were initiated when it was decreed that people were allowed three weeks each year to visit shrines. For sites venerating certain supersaints, bonus days or weeks were allowed. For travel to and from the holiest of holy places, Jerusalem itself, an entire year was allotted.

Today, the true art of pilgrimage is remembered as myth. But acknowledging the importance of myth may put us in touch with a visionary purpose in ourselves. Perhaps the heroism we honor in the saints or the movie stars will be born in our own souls as we participate in a trip somewhere—anywhere. Perhaps a wondrous action or insight will be birthed at a particular place. Perhaps we will return home more humble or more alive. Or, because we've dared to travel, we'll live with greater clarity. Travel as adventure and pilgrimage is simply making a visit to places where God is among us.

prolifically about refusing to "abandon the wild" within us. Her contributions to journalism focused on the idea of woman as intermediary between the land and contemporary political affairs. Developing the significance of female energy in particular, her work was called by the *New York Times* "the kind of continuous . . . adventure that makes a life into a pilgrimage."[7]

The high road, the road less traveled, is usually not at all smooth. Don't expect it to be laid out like wide Roman trade routes of marble mosaic that once wound through Europe and the Middle East. Yet upon this bumpy road you'll pay attention to what really matters. Your creative spirit matters. Activating your dream matters. Honing your resilience matters. Barbara Sjoholm concluded that travel is the state of being homeless and proclaims confidently, "We should welcome the opportunity it gives us to live nowhere."[8]

All travel is a quest, conscious or unconscious searching for something that is lacking in our lives or ourselves.

Freya Stark

When I worked at a Christian receiving home for "misfits" in Essex, England, I was, by virtue of being American instead of English, treated like one of the residents instead of like a staff member. When my youngest daughter, Lissa, ventured to Baja alone to work at a Mexican orphanage, she expected to be supported by the spirit of Christian fellowship. Instead, she encountered a clique of teenage volunteer girls who by their passive-aggressive behavior assaulted her emotionally and left her isolated. When my oldest daughter, Tirza, went to London for a semester abroad, her host family were vegans, who not only do not eat meat but do not allow it in the house. Not understanding the full scope of that, Tirza once bought a package of salmon cream cheese and placed it in the refrigerator. To her dismay, her host mom blew a cork and required that she wash down the refrigerator inside and out, as well as scrub the kitchen walls, all the kitchen furniture, and every cupboard.

Adventure will sometimes discomfort us, often through the barbs of other people. But "if you judge people [even people who judge you]," warned Mother Teresa, "you have no time to love them." Loving people, in fact, may be all the adventure you can stand! So is discovering that the joke is on you and laughing anyway. Women who arrived on the American frontier found the presence of native peoples disturbing even though most of the Indians approached the settlers with peaceful intentions. A Kansas pioneer wrote, "My windows were open and I was combing my hair . . . then very long, thick and even. As I drew the comb through it and looked up to the mirror before me, opposite the window, I saw reflected two big Indians, one had just gotten inside and the other was climbing over the window sill. I thought, of course, they were after my scalp. I screamed and ran. . . . The Colonel came into the room and found the Indians laughing heartily."[9] I wonder if she laughed too. Such are the discomforts of leaving one place and going where you've never gone before. If nothing else, it will always leave you with stories to tell.

In Frank Baum's tale *The Wizard of Oz* and Hans Christian Andersen's fairy tale *The Red Shoes*, we recognize the theme of female pilgrimage. The metaphor of special slippers as both empowerment and protection for the wearer has everything to do with adventure. If these young women were not on their way somewhere, bare feet would do. Adventure requires the appropriate footwear, because you are going to traverse a different kind of territory.

Travel surveys show that, after toothpaste and cell phones, women put shoes at the top of the list of items they would never leave behind on a trip. In the Middle Ages, pilgrims considered the most important things to have on any journey a wide-brimmed hat, a long walking stick, and a pair of heavy sandals. Thousands of years before, King Solomon praised his beloved, a shepherdess, by declaring, "How beautiful are your feet in sandals."[10] Surely, her feet had covered many miles of winding trails. Why this poetic commentary on their sensual appeal? Perhaps because from ancient times, the foot and footwear have been symbols of pilgrimage. I wonder, what could be more romantic?

One writer claims that adventure demands that we "put the soles of our shoes to the soul of the world."[11] The Hebrew people certainly lived this out. Moses blessed their tribes before his death, admonishing the most blessed of the twelve to dip his foot in oil. Was this to anoint the people for the many miles of travel ahead? After forty years in the wilderness, the Hebrews' sandals had not worn out.[12] Their footwear was durable, able to withstand the rugged journeys and battles. Later, the prophet Isaiah wrote that the feet of those who proclaim peace and bring good tidings—a great reason for travel—are nothing less than beautiful.[13] The apostle John, writing from exile, had a vision of an angel whose feet were like pillars of fire.[14] Shoes, and particularly fiery-colored shoes, image the adventure of humankind and the heavenly.

Our feet, clad in protective shoes, are what enable us to participate fully in our own adventures. So let us step beyond the mundane. Grab your hiking boots or strappy sandals—red or not. Know that something extraordinary will be required of you. Your shoes will get scuffed. Your feet may get blisters and be sore, achy, and surely, tired. But we'll explore our resourcefulness and God's grace even as we gaze upon the wonders of the world.

Finding Your Voice as a Stranger

I've often found myself not fitting in, not speaking the language, being an oddball or the odd man out. Being an introvert makes it harder for me to make friends or find my voice as a stranger among people of other cultures. But being an introvert will not stop me from traveling, even on my own. If you ever find yourself in a similar situation, listen to my experience; I hope it may offer help.

I've been the "ugly American" by default—when I lived in Denmark during the early 1970s, after Watergate, and during the scorned Reagan administration. I've also been the "beautiful American"—in England just after the movie *Love Story* premiered, when I wore my hair long and straight and, being tall like the movie's star, Ali McGraw, my American accent bought me some respect.

Finding a voice—your own voice—and feeling good about being you is necessary in good times and bad. What are you going to do to reverence what you know to be true and remember who you are wherever you are? Here's a start:

Journal daily. Talk to your inner woman, your little girl, your wild center, and God. Make sure you're dead honest with yourself. Listen to yourself talk back, and honor everything you have to say to yourself.

Be kind to yourself. Don't withhold and deny yourself simple pleasures. A ninety-some-year-old lady said, "If I had it to do over again, I'd pick more daisies." Give yourself a treat, take a bubble bath or an extra ten minutes to soak. Take a walk in the woods—or in the rain. Make a long distance call to someone you love. Cheat on your diet. Pick more daisies!

Reach out and touch someone. Be observant of others who may feel discouraged or appear to be disadvantaged. A smile is the same in any language. Offer friendship or just your presence to someone you don't know. Find ways to say, "I'm approachable."

Show a willing heart. You may be expected to act not as one from your own culture but as one from the culture you are visiting. Many people don't comprehend the differences or have never been exposed to other cultures. Basically, it's up to the foreigner to fit in with the place and people whose hospitality she is enjoying. Find something you like and participate in it. Attempt to speak the language and show you are willing to learn. Respect customs, even those contrary to your own.

Listen. Listen more. Listen well. Use eye contact. Hear every word without thinking about what you're going to say next. Give people the benefit of the doubt—mostly (true, there are some cons out there!)—and remember that everybody has a battle to fight. Listening is the holy ointment that soothes, heals, and builds again.

Above all, do not lose your desire to walk everyday. . . . I have walked myself into my best thoughts, and I know of no thought so burdensome that one cannot walk away from it.

Søren Kierkegaard

Walking the Via Dolorosa was never a spiritual objective of mine. But since I was invited on a tour for journalists during Passover in 1996, I joined pilgrims from around the world winding through the narrow streets of Old Jerusalem to visit the stations of the cross. We'd been warned of possible violence that day by the Hamas, a Palestinian terrorist organization. But, of course, you never think it will happen to you.

At the place where Christ fell, I took a photograph of my sandaled feet against the pavement to remind me of his identification with my own human vulnerability. Suddenly, Israeli soldiers, positioned on every corner, started shouting. Our guide went into action like a sheep dog, pushing us to run through a less-populated tunnel, away from the chaos that was arising. We stumbled past shops and finally into the sunshine outside the walls. There were no acts of terrorism that day, but the reminder of its ever-present possibility caused me to reflect upon the risks of even being alive at all. Why would I want to hold back? Why would I not want to participate in the adventure waiting for me?

My pilgrimage work on this earth is to coalesce everything I've ever been, done, thought, known, and experienced, as well as what I've wanted to do, where I've wanted to go, and all I've wanted to be. I am to keep my instincts, intuition, and imagination sharp by using them. I intentionally practice enthusiasm for its own sake, because I've proven that enthusiasm will take me farther than a good guidebook. I will articulate questions in the face of bewilderment and pray in the face of great danger or great love. Adventure is not just a way to enact faith for myself but an active way of giving back to the world part of its own lost faith.

Unpacking El Camino de Santiago

A Pilgrim's Profile: Patricia Danks

How I learned that what we stress about
from day to day is not the important stuff

Maybe I am looking for part of my own lost or broken soul that
went missing. Pilgrimage drives us, but hill walking is what gets
us there ... it is a poetic and sensual experience. It is a spiritual
act; an art form ... require[ing] nothing but our two feet and a
willingness to engage the natural world with fresh senses ... [It]
may also be an important facet of working with the soul."

Frank MacEowen

The road to Santiago de Compostela is nearly five hundred
miles of often grueling terrain with a history to match its
mystique. Patricia Danks, a psychotherapist and family counselor
in Belleville, Michigan, says that engaging the challenge of the
trek is one of the most amazing things she has ever done. Her
purpose was to celebrate her sixtieth birthday and her fifth year

as a survivor of breast cancer. "The pilgrimage put me in touch with the essentials," she says. "It has become the reference point for everything else in my life."

According to legend, the apostle James came to northern Spain after Christ's death to preach the gospel for a time. Though he was martyred in Jerusalem, his remains were carried back to the place where he'd brought hope and love. The story is told that eight thousand years later, his gravesite was rediscovered by the bright glow of a star circled by lesser stars. A cathedral was built over the site, and since that time, many a pilgrim has made the arduous journey to "St. James of the Star Field," as the destination is called.

Over the foothills of the Pyrenees Mountains, across fields of poppies and lavender, up and down steep trails of gravel and huge rocks, through valleys of ripe cherries and dense eucalyptus forests, pilgrims have buffeted their boots and bodies for thousands of years. In the summer of 2002, Patty Danks joined their ranks. "I wanted to do something bigger than life," she says. "I told myself, 'This is too big for me, therefore I'm going to attempt it!' It was to be a time of solitude with God. I wanted to reflect back on my life and think about where I was going from there."

From the very beginning, it was difficult. Patty says she walked too hard and too fast for the first few days. After becoming sick, she was forced to delay the trek and stay three days in a hotel. "There was some consideration whether I should be doing this at all," she says, "but I became more dedicated to the idea, even if I had to crawl."

With a heat wave simmering in Europe that summer, temperatures hovered around a hundred degrees Fahrenheit, and it was even warmer on the mesa where she was walking. Facing the first treacherous climb after leaving Roncesvalles, Patty announced again, "I can't do this," and was tempted to stop once more.

A fellow pilgrim reminded her, "Don't look at the mountain. Look at the trail; keep your eyes right where your feet are."

"With that wisdom, I started again but at a different pace. I learned *my* pace," Patty adds. Pushing her body to the brink, as long as she was able to keep her eyes on the path and not try to look too far ahead, she was fine. Things evolved around the essentials: using a walking stick—or sometimes two—looking for shade, knowing how much water she had to drink, stopping to rest for a day or two once a week. "Like with life," she says, "you find your own pace, and you look not ahead at what you have to surmount but at the next step that is right in front of you."

Following the "fetches amarillos" (yellow arrows) pointing the way from village to village or city to city (sometimes along busy highways), Patty hiked about thirteen miles (twenty kilometers) a day, rising to start at 5:30 a.m. That's about six hours a day. "Sharing parts of the journey was a joy," she says, "but letting other pilgrims go ahead or drop behind was part of it too. Like in life, I share my journey with wonderful people, but the return to solitude and to my time with God is right for me." In solitude, Patty found the greater blessing.

With the early morning sounds of roosters and dogs, she passed ancient stone barns, rivers, and meadow land. Patty's sensibilities were heightened. She recalls seeing one of the crosses marking where others had died along the trail (hundreds of years ago or recently). She watched magnificent sunrises over the horizon. One morning, a church appeared inch by inch as its spire seemed to grow from the road, announcing a village deep in a valley. Another day, she struggled uphill to make her way to an ancient village after running out of water. She found it deserted and desolate. Here, as many a time, Patty's ingenuity and faith were tested.

"I became acutely aware of what was needed to survive," she says. "In fact, one night I realized that everything valuable to me I kept in my hat at night: sunglasses, sunscreen, a bottle of water, my locket, toothbrush, and passport. Algergues, or hostels, were found every five or six miles offering rest, a shower, and a dormitory bed for about three dollars a day. Most included a rustic kitchen. In the cities, hotels offered a pilgrim's menu and a more comfortable bed with private bath. There, Patty meandered through historic museums, enjoying medieval art or relics of the Middle Ages.

For Patty, the pilgrimage was, at its best, a way to be in touch with God as one can experience only beyond time and culture. The rhythm of walking or climbing hour after hour, day after day, mile after mile, week after week gave birth to a spiritual high.

Patty made it all the way, reaching—thirty-eight days after her ambitious start—what the ancient Spaniards once called "the ends of the earth." As one whose life was changed by the experience, Patty proclaims the pilgrimage a perfect metaphor for life. She says, "In our culture, there is so much noise in our lives. I learned that what we stress about from day to day is not important stuff."

The proof is in the pudding: Patty plans to return and walk the Camino again in 2006.

6

Respect the Unexpected

Detours Welcomed

Strange travel suggestions are dancing lessons from God.

Kurt Vonnegut Jr.

As we moved along," wrote historian Etheria in AD 384, "we came to a certain place where the mountains through which we were journeying opened out and formed an infinitely great valley, quite flat and extraordinarily beautiful. Across the valley there appeared Sinai, the holy mountain of God."[1]

At some point on each of our journeys, we will come to a "certain place" where everything difficult, or that obscures the way, opens out. There, beyond the beauty, will appear in some guise a holy mountain. Such a mountain, a metaphorical mountain, is meant for your eyes only. It is a gift, the glory of it totally unexpected and out of character with the terrain through which you travel. When Diana Mount trekked in Nepal (see the profile of a pilgrim on page 44), the highest point she reached was overlooking the base camp to Mount Everest, with the world's highest mountain in view across a snowy valley. But that wasn't the holy climax of her trip. She saw the holy later in the middle of that night: a starry sky in a silent, magnificent world, a world in which she'd been called to participate and to be happy.

On one of my journeys, the holy metaphor that startled me was not a mountain at all but a waterfall. Hitchhiking to the Dead Sea back in the days before the fancy resorts, there were no fences, no private property, no busy highways. My girlfriend and I simply asked the driver to stop (we'd hitchhiked) along the deserted road through the Negev. We climbed out, he drove on, and we went swimming in the buoyant salt water. Against the backdrop of the desert, no one heard our voices or our laughter. We dried off, then crossed the road and headed into the bluffs and foothills on the other side. Rocky cave formations and a few barely visible trails led through thick foliage to En Gedi where David, the shepherd boy, had hidden from King Saul more than five thousand years before.

Exploring the area, we eventually came across paradise—a waterfall that dropped thunderous shafts of water into a clear pool. Here was water to shower the salt off our bodies and the tarnish off our imagination. We splashed like children in a virgin garden. I still carry the wonder I felt at being part of that magical landscape. When I returned twenty-five years later, En Gedi had been made into a park with gravel trails, signs, and people everywhere. Today, the minerals of the Dead Sea and the Negev that we enjoyed at their most primitive are being harvested and sold as beauty-enhancing bathing salts, face masks, and lotions. Steamy bathing facilities offer a swim in the sea and a mud bath for a pretty penny. If the waterfall is still there, I wonder, do pilgrims still hear the holy thunder?

Money Saving Tips

Plenty o' water. Who needs to sit at a sidewalk café when you can sip spring water in a piazza, watching people pose for photos in the falling daylight? Drink H_2O instead of sugary colas that dehydrate. Every ounce of sugar or caffeine you consume will require another ounce of water. Water is also the best internal moisturizer you can buy—it even beats those fabulous Chanel lotions. Your skin and pocketbook will thank you.

Lunch with a view. Who needs restaurants when you can buy a baguette, brie, and a bunch of grapes to enjoy along the banks of a river? Bread is cheap and fresh year round almost anywhere. Fruit and raw veggies are essential to keep your digestive system in synch and usually easy to find and easy to eat. Other options are sidewalk sausage or falafel stands, roast chicken shops, and delis offering sandwiches to go. On a rainy day, you can dodge into a coffee shop, buy something to drink, and bring your munchies with you.

Go local; drive slow. Short of hitchhiking and some rail passes, auto trips are still the most economical way for independent travel. Set your own schedule. Change your mind while en route. Pause as often as you like or get to your destination without interruption. Gas prices may spike in the summer, but there are lots of places to visit using alternative modes of transport: see the San Juan Islands via the ferries, hike the Pacific Crest Trail, bicycle through Napa Valley.

Hostels, not hotels. Though I'm in my fifties, I love staying in youth hostels. The best-run I've seen are in Washington DC and on Martha's Vineyard. Yes, I've shared a dorm room with ditsy high school girls who talk all night, but I've learned to appreciate the experience with humor. Good ear plugs are essential, as are an eye shield, plastic thongs for the shower, and an easy-on, easy-off robe. Elder hostels offer a huge range of activities, tours, and accommodations.

Just go. When times are hard financially and options for travel seem sparse, don't give up. If you can go to the next town or across town, then go there. Do something you've never done before: canoe along the river, visit an art gallery, or swing at a playground. Act friendly. Find something you like in everyone. Be curious. Offer a smile. It's amazing what you'll get in return.

All journeys have secret destinations of which the traveler is unaware.

Martin Buber

"Expect the unexpected" is a cliché that's been used for everything from selling mouthwash or perfume to encouraging the down-trodden and discouraged. Yet, when on pilgrimage, when adventure becomes your stock in trade, the unexpected will be yours on a regular basis. No one can say what the unexpected, the "holy mountain" will be for you, of course. That is up to your sensibilities and spiritual discernment to apprehend. When Paula McDonald wanted to go look for wildflowers and mushrooms, she bought a trail bike to explore the spiderweb of logging roads around her Wisconsin summerhouse. "Deep along those overgrown roads," she writes, "I found abandoned houses instead—and abandoned lives. Depression-era loggers' homes suddenly and mysteriously left, some with dishes still on the table." Her epiphany? "You never know where a trail, or life, will lead."[2]

Another traveler, looking for abandoned cabins in a mountain valley, may come upon wildflowers and mushrooms instead, finding them an equally eloquent commentary on life. Who is to say which discovery holds more spiritual power, joie de vivre, or opportunity for self expression? It is the nut-wild, unruly hearts that reap the most from this kind of travel.

Do you seek beauty in what's ugly? Comedy in what's too serious? Commitment to the adventurer's life means treasuring whatever shows up. Seekers of the holy on the hard road stubbornly insist that poetry can be found anywhere in the world. And if they don't find it, they write their own.

Traveling in groups is not as conducive to the unexpected, especially when a guide is involved. I've done my share of both guided and solitary travel, as a young wannabe hippie of the early 1970s and as a middle-aged journalist. But if you like guided tours, look for discoveries of a more interior kind. On a tour of Turkey's religious sites, I eschewed touristy spots and venues, but our guide left us no time for individual exploring. In Iznik, however, three of us did manage to locate and surreptitiously contact a Christian man whose congregation held secret worship services in a basement. Our confidential interview with him fascinated, but it was not the highlight of my trip. Unexpectedly, my holy mountain was a show for tourists. Now that took me by surprise.

Witnessing the art form of the whirling dervishes gave me a metaphor that I've applied to numerous difficult situations in life. I was mesmerized, but not only by the grace of it. I was captivated by the idea of expressing divine joy by whirling as part of a large circle of other dancers and at the same time spinning around one's own center of gravity. The dervishes place hands straight to each side, one palm up and the other facing down, to represent reaching up to God and out to humankind. That they keep balance while spinning and circling for long periods, as in a trance, is beautiful and unnerving. This expression of spirituality is profoundly divergent from how I was raised—namely, not to dance! With the dervishes, who are Sufis, the mystic arm of Islam, dance is used to express godliness. The full, floating white gowns and red cone hats tilted to one side become a charming—and, for me, disarming—metaphor for joy in prayerful movement.

Another surprise was in store for me at the touristy belly dance show the next evening. Now, you wonder, how could this be spiritual? While feasting on the best of a Turkish banquet, we watched dancers of all ages perform the ancient oriental dance that originated in the harems, but not to entertain men. In fact, belly dance, as it's now called, was originally done only in the company of women to celebrate special events like weddings or

O Pioneer!

"Out in the 'short grass country' of western Kansas, when the pioneer days . . . are mentioned, we think of covered wagons, meager homestead fare, parched fields, sun-bonneted women who dared hardships, and bronzed, square-jawed Yankee[s] . . . who wrote history with the plow."

One of these was Susan Shelby McGoffin, who wrote from her diary on the Santa Fe Trail: "Oh, this is a life I would not exchange for a good deal. There is such independence, so much free uncontaminated air which impregnates the mind, the feelings, nay every thought, with purity. I breathe free without that oppression and uneasiness felt in the gossiping groups of a settled home."[3]

the birth of a baby. The undulating movements were originated to synchronize with the movements of childbirth. The dancing of female family was to encourage a healthy birth process. Not until Turkish dancers were brought to vaudeville in the 1920s did the dance become perverted into a sexualized sideshow for entertainment.

Even without knowing these facts, I seemed to find in the dancing a piece of myself that had long gone missing. Truthfully, it was not the sultry moves of arms and legs, the glittery fashion, or the erotic swing of the hips that moved me, but something primal and soulful. Only later did I begin to understand why. In our culture, says theologian and Christian philosopher Thomas Moore, "spiritual values can sometimes wound our sexuality." He sees widespread attention to sex in the American media as a symptom of our failure to find a positive place for sex in the culture at large. Society, he claims, might tone down its moralism and begin to create a public life that returns soul to sexuality.[4] I find great wisdom in his words, and an artful expression of innocence in oriental dance that has taken me somewhere I've never been.

I dislike feeling at home when I'm abroad.

George Bernard Shaw

As an adventurer and pilgrim, I am poised, listening for the unexpected deep within myself. With experience, I've become part of a great tradition of adventurers who are sometimes quirky and don't take things too seriously. In the act of travel, we move easily between the comfort of cherished beliefs to unknown territory. We try things on for size. The principles of travel embody the ability to see the poignant in just about anything. Adventurers are true promoters of God-consciousness who have made an art of expecting the unexpected, the God-thing, at any time.

Traveling as adventure is like a dance. At times you go forward, almost gliding; at other times you must walk backward very fast. It takes courage for a person to engage in this kind of choreographed spontaneity. I recognize you as this kind of person by the fact you are reading this book into the sixth chapter. Adventure is almost like a sixth sense; if you have it, you know it and you recognize it in others. If you are not yet a veteran traveler, take a word from Eugene Ware, who declared that all glory comes from "daring to begin."

Where are you going to go?

Do you have a vision for the unexpected?

Perhaps you are already sitting on a "holy" rock reading these words or relaxing in a wayside park by a marble fountain. By the sheer fact that you made a start, you have increased your credibility. You have verified the reality that you are an adventurer in the spirit of those who know that adventure is worthwhile in itself. If you don't know where you want to go, there are lots of ways to explore that. Sometimes it takes finding out first where you do not want to go. Taking one step at a time to explore the unfamiliar terrain requires patience—with yourself, first of all, and with the appearance of the holy. To be a travel virgin is to welcome the experience for the experience itself and not expect it to be perfect the first time out. The best adventurers are those who are best at being themselves.

Bold adventurers take just a few steps more when tempted to give up, turn back, or call it quits. When climbing Black Crater, one of the smaller mountains in the volcanic Cascades, I almost quit after hiking two-thirds of the way. I'd found a sumptuous vista to enjoy and told my party to go on ahead without me. While I was resting, another climber, coming back from the summit, paused long enough to engage me in conversation and to say, "Keep going. It's worth it!" I did reach the top, but the holy was not there; it was in my decision to keep going. The holy was the tremendous sense of achievement that decision gave me.

The adventurer, expecting the unexpected, is willing to allow bewilderment to be a welcomed friend. She knows that being lost isn't always a bad thing. She understands that exhaustion is a sign of a day well lived and evidence of the fact that she has given her all. Safety is not the end-all value, and comfort is not necessary. The adventurer wants to see what's on the other side of the rock wall, the wide river, the gaping crevice. The pilgrim takes her meaning and ambience with her wherever she goes. She can put up with bad service or hard sleeping surfaces, because her mission is way bigger than any of those inconveniences and she is about to live heaven on earth.

The obituary for a woman named Bambi Homes, who died of cancer, included the following lines: "Each journey filled [Bambi] with wonder and confirmed her conviction that an open heart accompanied by an open mind was the most important passport a person could carry. Having recently returned from a raft trip down the Colorado River, she delighted in a motto a guide yelled as they ran Lava Falls: 'If you are not living on the edge, you are taking up too much space.'"[5] What more is necessary?

A friend once said to me about my dangling on the dangerous pinnacle of single parenting, "You live on the fray," as if that was something undesirable. Single parenting certainly requires living on the fray, and anybody who has done it knows what I mean. But I think about my friend's statement. With my children now raised, living on the fray is still my chosen lifestyle. I decided a long time ago to live on purpose. To throw all the paint possible on the canvas of life. To go get what I wanted—which is not an opulent lifestyle, money in the bank, or beautiful clothes, but the holy, that one treasure that comes most unexpectedly.

> Often while traveling with a camera, we arrive just as the sun slips over the horizon of a moment, too late to expose the film, only time to expose our hearts.
>
> Minor White

My grandmother Daisy left her home in Missouri during the Victorian era and traveled to Catalina Island, off the coast of Southern California, to work in a gift store—unheard of at that time for a single woman in her midtwenties. Earlier, at age sixteen, she had traveled to Tucson, Arizona, which at that time was famous for outlaws and bandits, to teach in a one-room schoolhouse.

My grandmother Leah seemed more stoic and staid. She was a wispy, delicate girl, understated and plain. But Kansas prairie women were indomitable. Some of them were rascals, like Carry Nation, who invaded saloons with an ax. Kansas women assumed responsibility to tame the middle of nowhere and make it the middle of somewhere: plumb center of the USA. The Kansas state motto, *Ad Astra per Aspera*, "To the Stars through the Wilderness," says it all.

103

Overseas Travel Tips

Pare down your wardrobe. Clothing of soft fabrics that can be tightly rolled and easily washed by hand is essential. For example, a long skirt and a short skirt, one pair of shorts, an extra pair of pants (khakis or jeans), and a few basic tops will take you anywhere in Europe. Use light nylon underwear that can be washed out and dried overnight. Roll like items (to minimize wrinkles) and stack them tightly into gallon-size ziplock bags where you can overview what you have.

Wear a pair of top-quality, sturdy sandals, shoes, or boots in a classic style. You won't need any other footwear, which can be bulky and heavy to carry. Paint your toes red for a summer concert and you'll always feel dressy. Break in new shoes several weeks prior to your trip so they fit to perfection. A pair of rubber thongs comes in handy for the shower or beach.

Take one comfy, fleecy jacket you can tie around your hips when not needed and can sleep in if necessary on a cold night. An envelope-size fold-up plastic parka with hood can be tucked into a pocket so you won't need a clumsy umbrella (sew an inside chest pocket into your jacket for it).

Let your back carry the pack. I traveled twenty-one days with a small (two feet by one foot) backpack and never got sore shoulders or had to stop and rest on long walks to the station, hotel, or sights. (I Velcroed extra foam pads under the shoulder pieces.) Choose a pack with lots of exterior pockets for toiletries, makeup, hair essentials, a book, and a bottle of water. The pack will often come in handy as a backrest too. If you do take a suitcase, make it a small roll on; you'll have to carry it over cobblestones and many bumpy sidewalks.

Carry a plastic thermal coffee mug. Some regions, like southern Europe, charge exorbitant prices for a small cup of java. I clipped my mug to the outside of my backpack. I would request hot water at sidewalk cafés (I was never asked to pay for it), then step outside and mix my own brew of instant coffee and creamer. Another option is to carry a small (one-cup size) French coffee press (available at most department stores). The glass is sturdy, but you'll have to be a little more careful. Buy your grounds at home, not overseas.

Invest in a Bucky travel pillow. The lightweight, u-shaped neck pillow carries or packs well. Clip it to your backpack or belt and you'll be surprised how often you use it. Wrap it around your neck on the flight, sit on it for long trips on hard seats, cushion your head on a nap in a park. My stylish daughter laughed at me for taking one when we left on our trip across Europe. By midtrip she was sheepishly asking to borrow it, and by the end was sneaking it every chance she could!

I honored the legacy of my grandmothers, adventurers in their own right, when I decided to change my last name. Not wanting to go back to my maiden name (Smith), I composed my own, a combination of Leah and Daisy, LeDai, speaking to me of the adventurous spirit, underestimated, possibly undervalued, possessed by women who knew what it was to live as pilgrims on this earth.

In medieval times, there were no signposts or maps on the roads to pilgrimage sites. Travelers rarely followed the infamous Roman roads made for marching armies. Most had to rely on memorized directions or a guide. They traveled in detours and zigzags. Sometimes pyramids of stacked stones called "montjoies" showed the way. Other times bells were rung from the monasteries to call the stray. To get lost meant probable death. Boatmen were warned against as enemies. Bridge tolls were high. Crossing any mountain ranges meant encountering the complication of foreign languages. Yet under all these dangerous circumstances, adventurers of all ages were characterized by their respect for the unexpected.

"How could they put into words the way it felt to have conquered the solitude and anguish," it has been asked of women adventurers, "to have reached on the physical plane the most elusive of all spiritual goals: the transcending of capability?"[6] I believe this question, put to us by the editors of *Women of Discovery*, is most beautiful. Living this question is the grail we find when we set sail for unknown places within and without ourselves.

Part 3

A Time
for Epiphanies

7

A Woman's Perspective

Place Changes You

I want to do it because I want to do it. Women must try to do things as men have tried. When they fail, their failure must be a challenge to others.

Amelia Earhart

Travel author Marybeth Bond tells of how, while hiking through Himalayan villages, most of the men focused their cameras, snapped their pictures, and hiked quickly on. "The women, on the other hand, lingered," she writes. "They moved in closer, made eye contact (most often with other women), sometimes cooing over a child or . . . rocking a baby."[1] Even travel industry studies show how differently women and men travel. Researchers note that men look for ways to conquer a mountain or utilize it in recreation. Women, on the other hand, look for landscapes with ambience and contact with people. While men want to go places where they can somehow make their mark, women seek out places they've never been before. Men want to take part of a place home as a trophy, while women want to observe scenic beauty and reflect upon it.

With the popularity of women's travel "going through the roof,"[2] the travel industry has revised its marketing plan. They are now plotting to deliver the goods women want. Experts say women look to be "transformed," because they are conscious that the inner landscape is as important as the outer landscape. They want to participate in the world rather than change it or possess it. A woman wants to share her own persona, and that she does—by letting a place change her. Author Kathleen Norris, originator of the term *spiritual geography*, puts the feminine viewpoint of travel so beautifully when she discerns that you have only to let "place" happen to you.

When I lived in Salzburg, I instinctively absorbed its charming and colorful sense of place. I snapped photos of men and boys in worn lederhosen laboring in the city. Enchanted by women and girls in their fairy-tale Bavarian-style dresses, I had a dress made for myself and wore it out and about every day, just like the locals. I took German classes and learned to offer with gusto the local dialect greeting, *Grussgott!* At Christmas, I attended a concert in the nearby village of Oberndorf where Franz Gruber and Joseph Mohr wrote "Silent Night" and performed it for the first time in 1818. I munched on Lebkuchen (gingery cookies) while browsing bright holiday stalls of hand-painted decorations. In spring, I walked countless trails through the lower slopes of the Alps. I skied, picnicked, browsed in the windy cobbled streets. Summer days off were usually spent wandering about the towered castle on the hill and below it, through Mirabelle gardens, lunching on steamy sausages at street corners.

When I left Salzburg one year later, I wondered, *Am I leaving myself behind? Have I become part of the landscape too? Did I*

Taking Readers on a Tour

Want to write about what you've experienced on the open road? Here are some tips to start you on the path to publishing them:

Always query the publication you want to write for. Simply send a letter, like an invitation to an editor, to outline your idea and what you believe readers will get from it. Include a self-addressed stamped envelope if using snail mail. A query reserves your space to submit on that place or topic within a reasonable period of time.

Crystallize the idea you are selling (brief writing is best writing), identify why it's hot, and when writing your query, offer ideas that are specific to the publication's readership.

Give your publishing history and include a copy of one or two previously published articles or sample stories. Identify your unique sources or skills. Include information about any photos you are prepared to supply.

Showcase your stuff like posh window dressing in New York City: the originality of your article idea and your fabulous writing style should sell itself in the query. Create a brief, concentrated appeal with vivid images, maximum one page. Rework it until it shines like nothing else you've ever written.

If going to a popular place, include a twist in your query: instead of detailing what to do on Maui, tell how to spiff up your stay at the Best Western and recreate like a queen on the budget of a beggar. Come up with ideas by putting your own spin on common travel themes. Wonder: What would the Gospels look like written from the perspective of a female disciple? How do you visit a concentration camp like Auschwitz? What did you learn about God through the eyes of Dutch painters? Interview the homeless instead of the politicians.

Use vivid, not vapid, language. Instead of describing water as muddy, show us the color of it: "like Turkish coffee grounds in the bottom of a glass cup." Let your wild side out to play. Think backward or at least out of the box. Play the devil's advocate. Take risks.

Remember that timing matters; don't take rejections personally. One magazine may have just purchased a story of a woman snowboarding in Switzerland. Overlapping article ideas or a plethora of articles on the same idea is the most common reason for rejection. Keep sending out multiple queries, hitting a number of targets at one time.

A reply may offer a specific direction or angle on the topic; that's wonderful! If you're open to being a catalyst for editorial ideas, you'll anticipate the editor's perspective. You'll offer editors what they do not yet know they want. Accept the new directions where possible and go with the flow. Building relationships with editors may establish your career in a certain niche.

give anything back? Unlike my friend Helen, who left a beautiful garden at the B & B where we worked, or Les the handyman, who left the house in tip-top shape, I had washed and ironed innumerable sets of linens, fluffing feather-downs and hanging them on balconies to air in the crisp mountain air. But what had I left there besides my heart, torn at leaving?

Look at every path closely. . . . Then ask yourself . . . one question. . . . Does this path have a heart?

Don Juan's advice to Carlos Castaneda

In travel, you often end up in places so unexpected that even the most ordinary adventures seem magical, says Thalia Zepatos. Magical? Certainly, Salzburg is magical, but what about the mundane? What about a business trip to downtown Detroit, Michigan? When you go somewhere—anywhere—the magic of a place really comes from within yourself. I have a friend, Catrina, in the local women's penitentiary who inspires me. If there ever was a dark and depressing place, she is in it 24/7. But when she walks into the plain gray room where we meet each week for Bible study, it changes; it takes on personality. I wonder, why are her bright eyes and sunny smile so different from the faces of other inmates who also attend the study? She shares the same facilities and limitations with them. All these women are trapped within the same walls.

Catrina's secret is subtle: she carries the ambience and the joy within her. If this unexpected detour behind bars is not worse than mundane, I don't know what is. Yet her world, even in prison, is wide open, because Catrina sees something others don't, something that comes from within herself, placed there by the grace of God.

Just as pilgrimage was being rediscovered at the turn of the new millennium, it was nearly shut down by the terrorist attacks of

September 11, 2001. On a national level, Americans, in general, are now traveling less overseas and more within the boundaries of our own continent. But true adventurers are creating new ways to explore time-tested places and see them in new ways. Did you grow up in the Midwest? The Northeast? The South? How about a pilgrimage to revisit, for good or bad, the places you remember. They will have changed like you have. But it is what you bring with you that counts to make even weathered or commercialized places retain significance.

Bring something to commemorate your connection to a place. Donate a book to the local library, the one you loved to visit as a child. Take part in a clean-up campaign in the downtown district. Lay flowers on the graves of family members who have passed on. If you visit some of our national treasures, like Yellowstone National Park, the cliff dwellings of the Anasazi people in Northwest Arizona, or the lighthouses along the rugged coastline of Oregon, find a personal way to participate in their mystique. As the saying goes, take nothing but memories and leave nothing but footprints. Let the place happen to you and leave with graffiti on your own soul.

I am exploring the human condition rather than physical space.

Christiane Amanpour

When I visited Washington DC, before 9/11, with my middle daughter, Leyah, I was basically along for the ride, doing whatever she wanted to do. One morning, we realized we would not be able to visit the White House because the lines were too long. Instead, we visited the Lincoln Memorial and were walking back along the reflecting pool, when Leyah skipped out into the water to pick up some candy wrappers floating there. By the time we reached the end, she had a handful. Then we noticed a well-dressed man approaching us, definitely not a tourist. I wondered if we were going to be scolded for Leyah's wading through the pool.

The man approached us with a big smile and simply asked if we'd like him to take our photo together. He commented that he enjoyed seeing people take pride in our nation's capital. "I get so tired in the office," he said, "I have to get out and watch people to remind myself why I'm still here." Then he added, "By the way, may I invite you to the White House and a tour of the State Department?"

"Oh, are you a guard there?" I stammered.

"I've worked for five presidents," he told us, handing us his business card bearing the words "Office of the President." After a fascinating conversation, Leyah and I arranged to meet him the next morning at the White House. He escorted us to the head of the line and introduced us like old friends to the guards stationed at the door. After the White House tour, he met us at the entrance to the State Department next door and took us on a personally escorted tour of the offices on all floors. I was still in awe when upstairs we passed a long line of doors from which large padlocks were hanging. When we asked what those rooms were, our new friend told us that inside, the president's cabinet was discussing the situation in Kosovo. This was 1999, just after the U.S. bombings had begun.

Leyah, who had just finished her high school social studies class, blurted out, "Oh, I have to go talk to those people!" Our friend got nervous, then paused when he saw Leyah walk quietly over to one of the doors and gently lay her hand on it. In a moment of silence, she closed her eyes as if unashamed to make herself part of history.

Next, our friend led us into a plush office, right past the secretaries, into the inner sanctum. "I want you to meet a friend of mine," he told me. I noticed family pictures on the large desk in

Creating a Sketchbook Journal

A dominant impulse on encountering beauty is to wish to hold onto it, to possess it and give it weight in one's life. There is an urge to say, "I was here, I saw this and it mattered to me."

Alain de Botton

An essential component of the unforgettable journey is documentation. Forget about laborious diaries—your trip shouldn't be spent between the pages of a book. And you don't need to keep that camera glued to your eye anymore. This is about sensing a breathing, three-dimensional world. Although a few photographs are helpful to remind you of the trip and to share it with others, a travel journal preserves the experience itself. With a little creativity, you can create a timeless memoir during the inevitable waiting around that travel often entails.

Before your trip, buy a sturdy unruled journal small enough to fit into your day bag. A spiral-bound book works well, because you don't have to hold it open as you use it. Pick up a few colored pencils or one of those miniature watercolor sets made for children. Don't forget a glue stick and several fine-pointed permanent pens.

Your journal begins on day one with the first ticket stub. Or you might glue in a small section of a map to show where you're going. Glue in labels from something new you ate or flowers you pressed the day before. Cut out photographs from visitors' pamphlets. Don't worry if something sticks out of your book—the bulkier the better. Keep a sharp eye for wrappers, postcards, and feathers to add as you build your narrative hope chest of the journey. Alongside these pieces of "hard evidence," write in your emotions or expectations for the trip. You want this journey to bring you face-to-face with personal goals.

A snapshot may hint at something, but only a drawing will capture that subject as your own living memory. If you're intrigued by a strange leaf, put your pen to a blank page and let it follow your leaf as you imagine an ant walking around its perimeter. And if, at the very worst, all you create are incoherent marks on paper, they'll reveal the anxiety or calm of the moment. Although, gluing or painting over them is allowed—there are no rules! Rubbings add artwork also; just lay a page over an inscription and rub away with a pencil.

Allow your handwriting to break all conventions—let it sprawl across both pages as you float on a river, or spiral as words describe a church. Switch between cursive and all caps.

Consider having people you meet fill in blank spaces with their addresses. And if there are children around, don't miss an opportunity to let them decorate your journal with pictures of their own! Drawing is a great way to communicate with children who speak a different language and a great alternative to photographing them, which sometimes causes tension.

Cover the outside of your journal with local fabric or a map. It should be wrapped like the treasure it is: a sensual walk back through adventure.

Leyah Jensen

the floral-patterned office, then suddenly recognized them as the Al Gore family. Our friend said, "Oh, too bad. Tipper's not here right now. I really wanted her to meet you." I stood with my mouth agape. I was standing in the office of the wife of the vice president of the United States of America. Now it was my turn to pause and stand a few moments in her office to absorb the fact that just being there at all was somehow a moment of destiny. You never know what may happen when you offer yourself to a place.

More often than not you'll discover that adventure is a decision after the fact—a way of deciphering an event or an experience that you can't quite explain.

Rolf Potts

In the Middle Ages, shrines, not political institutions, were the sacred real estate of the age and the destination of sightseers. Women were their primary customers, serving as essential contributors to the economy right down the social scale. A whole population lived off the pilgrims, just like today. This population included toll takers, innkeepers, money changers, priests, guides, souvenir vendors. With women's full access to popular relics, some saints catered to a distinctly feminine clientele. Sir Thomas More poked gentle fun at housewives of the early sixteenth century, accusing them of spending more on pilgrimage to St. Zita to petition for lost keys than the keys were worth. But women's participation didn't stop with tourism; along the way women pilgrims nursed the sick and stopped to minister to other pilgrims.[3]

Isn't tourism itself somehow tangled with the idea of our search for spiritual healing? When visiting the cemetery at Saint-Laurent-sur-Mer above Omaha Beach with 150 World War

II veterans, it was not my goal to scoop up a bit of sand in a bottle to commemorate my father's participation in D-Day or to buy historic memorabilia. My mission was to interview the men who had been there in 1944, crawling their way through the hedgerows to the next village, and the next, under gunfire. As they wandered forty-five years later among the graves, their silence told it all.

Local people turned out in droves to look into the faces of the men who had liberated them from Nazi occupation. A French woman told me she was four years old when Nazi soldiers came through her village taking her family's only blankets and all their dried meat. When the Americans landed months later, she hid in the back room, shivering with fear once more. To her surprise, the Yankees handed out oranges, chocolate, and blankets in the streets. Later, they played softball in the streets with neighborhood boys, leaving behind their laughter. For her, the arrival of American veterans forty-five years later was an opportunity for pilgrimage back to her childhood village and a way to say thank you for the first time.

American veterans and family members were greeted by hundreds of school children dressed in their Sunday best at Henri Chapelle cemetery in Belgium. Each child held an American flag in one hand and a bouquet of flowers in the other. Each of them came up to one of us and led us through a beautiful archway into a cemetery stretching on for acres, row upon row of white crosses or stars of David bearing the names of thousands of American soldiers. Each of us was taken to the grave of one soldier, where we placed the flag and the flowers. I wrote down the name and birth and death dates of the man whose life was being honored by the Belgian child with me. Some of the children knelt at the gravesides, while others stood respectfully for a moment of silence.

Once home from my trip, I wrote an article about that place, wondering if the man at whose grave I'd stood had left a family,

117

The Best Advice Ever

On my very first trip abroad, someone gave me a piece of advice that has never been surpassed in wisdom. I pass it on, knowing you'll find it helpful wherever you are: Whatever happens, laugh about it!

Laughing is the best-kept secret of a successful trip. Don't get offended by anything. Don't take anything personally. Don't try to settle the score. Don't criticize, condemn, or complain. Chill. Stay calm. Keep cool. Nobody can make you feel bad unless you give them permission to, so don't!

If something unpleasant happens, be like a two-year-old just learning to respond to the world. When you stumble and fall or someone makes an unjust criticism of you, just laugh. Laugh fully. Laugh heartily. Laugh lightly. Get over it. Move on. Research shows that even if you force your mouth into a grin, you release endorphins into your blood stream. Let the endorphins roll.

Think positive. If you're going to err, let it be on the side of optimism. Stop thinking of all the miserable things that could happen. Expect the best. When bad things occur—and they will—you've made up your mind ahead of time to laugh. So do it. Even a forced laugh will do you good. Behave your way into the feelings that laughter conjures. Was there a mix-up in reservations and all the beds are taken on the overnight ferry to Corfu? Laugh. You'll spend a miserable night trying to stretch out on the deck chairs or the floor, but you will never forget it! And you'll have a story to tell.

Laugh. You'll have more fun. And so will everybody you're traveling with.

children, or a farm. Within weeks of the article's publication in a magazine, I received a letter from a woman in Illinois telling me that her nephew had read the article in a doctor's office. The nephew had immediately called her, wondering if the grave was that of his uncle, her brother. She'd been awestruck to read her brother's name in the article and see a photograph of his grave. The soldier's story came full circle, and so did the story of my trip.

If you think you can, you can. And if you think you can't you're right.

Mary Kay Ash

In the context of travel, women support and celebrate each other, seeking an experience that will connect them more closely to the human condition. But as relationship-oriented beings, we are sometimes most in need of initiating, or at least allowing, transformative experiences for ourselves. In her trek across Australia's outback by camel, Robyn Davidson's perspective was one of self-conquest. "If I could bumble my way across a desert," she wrote in *Tracks*, "then anyone could do anything. And that was true especially for women, who have used cowardice for so long to protect themselves that it has become a habit . . . build[ing] fences against possibility."[4]

Pilgrimage for women starts with the attitude that we are all pilgrims on this earth, sojourners with a high calling. We are reaching for altitude, and when we reach it, we become women with attitude. We summon significance to the surface in our travel, playful or solemn. We cross boundaries both within ourselves and on the maps we study. We get up and make our own adventure, provoking ourselves beyond perceived limits. In the process, we release our creative energy for the benefit of others.

In the early nineteenth century, St. Therese Couderc, for example, started a retreat house movement as the church in France was beginning to wake up after the disarray of the revolution. Since there had been no suitable place for women pilgrims to stay (they were usually housed with men sleeping on straw in crowded churches), Couderc created a prototype for pilgrim lodgings as places of spiritual and personal growth.[5]

As adventurers—unlike sightseers with map and guidebook in hand—we often don't know what we are looking for until we find it. Sometimes we arrive back home never having found that

119

special something. We may wonder about the purpose of our trip and yet possess a sense that something even better happened than we'd hoped. Perhaps we helped heal others. Perhaps we ourselves were healed. Perhaps the trip taught us to laugh more often or to laugh at ourselves. Such experiences may eventually spur us on to further travel.

One thing I know for certain. In the years following any adventure, we will finally understand that as women, one of our highest callings is to value our own open-ended stories and find a way to share them. Like St. Therese Couderc, we must be able to say, "My heart embraces the whole world."

Unpacking the Baja

A Pilgrim's Profile: Katie Emrich

How I learned that we can all be
ambassadors in this world when fear
doesn't hold us back

A [wo]man of ordinary talent will always be ordinary, whether
[s]he travels or not, but a [wo]man of superior talent . . . will go
to pieces if [s]he remains forever in the same place.

Wolfgang Amadeus Mozart

Born and raised an only child, Katie Emrich grew up chasing lynx in the Canadian wilderness, pretending she was Sacagawea. Once married with five children, "roadblocks, bumps and potholes" kept her from the great outdoors and all the things she loved to do. Staying true to her love for nature and following her dreams later brought concern from family members. Katie says, "A lot of people told me, 'You can't do that.' I did it anyway

121

because at fifty-seven years old you've got to do the things that feed your soul or you end up being sick. Pure and simple."

Katie, of Sisters, Oregon, wants to encourage any woman who thinks she can't do the things she's dreamed of doing. "It may be because other people believe she's not supposed to, or because she doesn't have enough money, or because she is afraid," Katie says. "You may see the bad things going on in the world, and yes, you might be in harm's way; that's how I feel every time I cross that border between California and Mexico. But don't just stay home. We can all be ambassadors in the world!"

Katie didn't pay attention to her own creative needs until a relationship ended in heartbreak. She decided she had to do something to heal herself. "I decided, I've got to get closer to my soul," she says. She saved money and bought an airplane ticket to San Jose, in Baja, California. An American friend, who'd been inviting her for ten years to visit, picked her up and drove her the hundred miles back to a beautiful strip of coastline near a small village.

"The first evening, I walked the quarter mile to the beach," Katie explains. "The sun started to go down—I'm a painter—and the sky turned watermelon, peach, and violet. I just sat there and bawled. Here was this palate of color on the Sea of Cortez. That white sand and those waves! I was sitting in the sand and all I could do was cry."

Katie tells how a young Mexican woman sitting about fifty feet away from her got up, came over, and spoke to her in Spanish. "I couldn't understand," she says, "because all I knew was *Hola* and *Adios*. But I realized she just wanted to see if I was okay." She was a school teacher in the village, and she and Katie became the best of friends. "That's how I came to volunteer teaching art in that village and other schools," she says. "They had nothing. I took art supplies in a suitcase." Katie also painted scenes of Baja life and sold them locally or to collectors who knew her from galleries in the U.S.

"I liked that place so well, I went again the next year," Katie says. That's when she met Carl, an American fisherman from her hometown. "We fell in love." Together, they returned to Baja every year, camping for two to five months a thousand miles below the border in a wilderness area by the sea. Eight years later, Carl died in Katie's arms. That next winter, Katie knew she had to go back to Baja without him. "I had to do it for me," she says. "I got in my truck and drove it alone all the way down.

"I've been back every year since then," Katie explains. "I share an authentic Mexican experience with Mexican friends I cherish. My experience is completely different than someone who goes to wine and dine in Cabo San Lucas. What I do is on the opposite end of the spectrum."

Even so, Katie struggles to put together the money to leave home after her landscaping season. Running a gardening business called the Garden Angel, Katie started with a pair of gloves in one pocket and a pair of clippers in the other. "My clients gave me the name," she explains, "because I paint pictures in people's yards instead of canvas, using flowers instead of paint." With money tight, Katie still uses a graph to plot her bills ahead, showing when to put money aside. When the graph is colored in with green, that means Katie's good to go.

Katie's friends sometimes fly in to join her. "I have a tent all ready with down comforters and pillows, and I build a fabulous outdoor kitchen every year. I even take my grandmother's glass stemware and china. In the evenings, sometimes twelve people from up and down the beach will gather—by candlelight—at my campsite right on the Sea of Cortez."

One year Katie took her thirteen-year-old son to spend five and a half weeks with her in the wilderness, joined later by her daughter. The next Christmas, the two children flew in for holidays full of swimming, painting, cooking, and hiking. Like their mother, Katie's kids don't mind doing without the comforts of home. Coming back from their first trip, Katie hit a sixty-five mile per hour crosswind. "In my rear view mirror, I saw the entire front of my old camper waving its metal at me," she says. "We stopped, hauled out the duct tape—'Mexican welding rod'—and taped it back together for the rest of the trip."

About three hours away from home that same trip, in the middle of nowhere she found the entire drive line of her truck lying on the ground. The u-joint had disintegrated! "So I bungee-corded it up," she says, "crawled the fifty feet to the shop, and slept right there." The mechanic replaced everything the next morning. Within an hour of home, she heard a terrible noise and found the bracket had broken around the rubber collar on the bearing. "I called my mechanic at home," she says, "and was told, 'Katie, you're going to have to use creative problem solving.'"

"Oh, I have Mexican welding rod!" Katie announced. Katie crawled under the truck and, winding strips of duct tape up and around, fashioned a bracket of her own.

Before her first trip to Baja, Katie says her dad almost disowned her out of concern for her safety. Last year, at age seventy-five, he visited Katie's Baja campsite for the first time. "He told me with tears in his eyes that he would never worry about me again," she says. "But next year, I'm doing something different. I'm going to Costa Rica with a backpack—I haven't told my dad yet!

"The world is an amazing place," Katie says. "The people I've met in Baja have forever enhanced the quality of my life. It would be hard to imagine not having gone the first time, not having opened this chapter in my life. Thank God I did not let fear hold me back."

8

The Mystique of Thin Places

Crossing Thresholds

When we look with the eyes of faith, all the ground we walk on becomes holy ground, all the people and all the common sights and sounds and happenings become miracles.

Herbert F. Brokering

In City Soleil, the thirty-six-square-mile slum of Port-au-Prince, Haiti, I step through mud, dodging pools of rancid green water. On the threshold of a cement-block house, a three-year-old looks after her two-year-old sister, feeding her one grain of rice at a time from a dirty cup. In a small hut nearby, a full-bellied teenage girl climbs onto a rusty metal bed covered by a piece of plastic. A man in dark trousers and shirt pulls on a pair of latex gloves, ready to deliver her baby. There is nothing else in the room except a bucket of water. In a "hospital" without bandages, toilet paper, or medicine, an old woman, her eyes filled with agony, holds a lethargic child against her own withered body. These otherworldly scenes fill me with intense emotion, and more, at what some women endure in their journey through life. In some places, the line between heaven and hell is very thin.

When you dare to go somewhere you have never been, you can expect to experience the "liminal," those spiritual thresholds where separation between the eternal and the everyday is indiscernible. The liminal, or "thin places," is an ancient Celtic idea that refers to a geographical location or a moment in time. It is the place where an unseen or ancient reality intersects with the obvious temporal reality. It is where the profane and the profound intertwine. When one is present in a thin place, the sacred can't be distinguished from the sentimental.

"We know that a dream can be real, but who ever thought that reality could be a dream?" asked Rod Serling in his introduction to 1960 TV's popular *The Twilight Zone.* "We exist of course, but how? In what way?" he asked week after week. I often watched the show and memorized those haunting lines. Through travel, I explore Serling's concept in a deeper way than staying home, because travel takes me outside familiar circumstances. What is real? "It is not necessarily at home that we best encounter our true selves," writes travel proponent Alain de Botton. (And, I would add, that we also best encounter the truth.) "The furniture insists that we cannot change because it does not; the domestic setting keeps us tethered to the person we are in ordinary life, who may not be who we essentially are."[1]

When we do take ourselves places we have never been, we may be shocked or saddened by other realities, as I was in Haiti, or we may be thrilled and exhilarated. But in any case, we usually begin to question who we are in relation to such realities. Liminal places, in particular, have a heightened potential to change us. Well-known places where this is true include the tomb of the unknown soldier in any country; the Sea of Galilee, where

Jesus walked and taught; Ground Zero in New York City; the pyramids of Egypt; the Grand Canyon.

In the 1991 movie *Grand Canyon*, expertly woven around the theme of violence and beauty, a wife reflects, whispering to her husband about wonderful and terrible events that changed their lives: "Something has happened, and you can't just go back and have it not happen. A connection has been made, and you have to play it out. What if these things are miracles and we don't have any experience with miracles so we're slow to recognize them?" When her husband tells her he has a headache, she says, "What if I'm right and these are truly miracles? Then it is inappropriate to get a headache in the presence of a miracle." Later, she wonders more about the thin places: "Everything is so close together. All the good or bad things in the world. Everything. I feel it in myself even, and in us."[2]

Immediately after seeing this movie, and being profoundly moved by it, I fittingly experienced a thin place of my own. Chatting with friends in a book café surrounded by large glass windows in Portland, Oregon, suddenly a loud bang rang through the room. Slowly, as if in surreal space, people quietly lowered their newspapers, magazines, and books. Everyone looked at each other in shock. Outside, someone standing at the bus stop shouted, "That white VW! A gun poked out the window and shot into the café!" Someone got up, went to the window, and found a small bullet hole. No one was hit, but I went home shaky that night, impressed by the veil between what may have ended tragically and an ordinary cup of coffee in a familiar place.

I touched the place and the place touched me.

James D. Houston

127

Dream Vacation Reality

Want to start your dream vacation right now? Here are some guidelines to help you identify where you want to go and why, set up some expectations, and begin to anticipate it. Nothing is impossible once you've taken the first step! The following are things you can do right now to jump-start the process.

Create a special notebook for your dream vacation and add to it as you develop ideas, come across articles or news clips about places, or simply change your mind. Have fun with the dreaming and it will move you into a place where you can receive what you most want. Make a list of up to five places you've dreamed of visiting. List them in order of priority according to your fascination with each place. Now think of one more dreamy place—somewhere you never thought you'd be able to go. A place you'd go if someone offered you a trip absolutely anywhere, all expenses paid. Answer the following questions for each place you've listed:

Who would I like to go with me? Or do I want to go on my own?
What is drawing me to this place?
What do I expect to see, learn, or experience there?
Where would I like to stay when I get there?
What am I feeling as I imagine myself in that place?
What is my most idealistic expectation of that place?
What is my worst fear about going/being
    there?
What kind of souvenir would I like to take
    home from there?

Continue to document your dream destinations by adding quotes, photos, and copies of articles you've read about them. Add new places or delete old ones. Notice which places rise to the top of your thinking and stay on your list. Keep working with this and watching for ways for the vacation to become possible. I guarantee you, it is!

For my father, the Vire River near Saint-Lô, France, is a thin place. Here, as a company commander in World War II, a young sergeant saved his life. The sergeant, after offering to jump first across an opening in the thick foliage while on a scouting mission, fell into the water when an enemy bullet found its target in his heart. When my father visited the river forty-five years later, it was dry, but my dad's eyes were not.

Celtic poet John O'Donohue writes that landscape is numinous. It "has a secret and silent memory," he says, "a narrative of presence where nothing is ever lost or forgotten."[3] This is true of the Vire River and also reminds me of the excavation under the Western Wall in Jerusalem. There is a place where the wall comes close to the foundation of Solomon's temple destroyed in AD 70, upon which the Dome of the Rock was built between 687 and 691. At this place along the wall, water seeps out of the rock despite the fact that there is no water source on the other side. Israelis simply say, "The wall is weeping."

Personal dwelling places also hold many thin places leading from past to present. These include the hearth where fires are kindled regularly throughout the day. Doorways where we say hello or good-bye many times each week. Areas of a dwelling where a sacred role is maintained—like a kitchen stove—or where suddenly something is changed with dramatic impact. The dining table after children are grown and gone may be considered a thin place.

My bedroom, and particularly my bed, was a thin place for me after my twenty-year marriage ended. It was here I struggled with demons in the night, read books of wisdom each morning, and journaled for hours in between. From this bed I documented emotions with a ferocity I had no idea I possessed. I scribbled fierce questions to a God in whom I wasn't certain I still believed. The bed, a symbol of love and commitment, had suddenly, with the beloved one's infidelity, became a symbol of betrayal. Once

I began to sleep in it alone and the days rolled by, it was washed by millions of tears. With the passing of years, it was hallowed by just as many prayers whispered within its comforting quilts. My bed was the place where I eventually began to hear the voice of God whisper back to me, a place separated from the kingdom of heaven only by an invisible curtain.

Raising my children alone, a privilege and an act of love, I began to recognize our home as characterized by many liminal spaces, like windows covered with my daughters' fingerprints. At the end of those ten years, I met the man of my dreams and found thin places in symbols of our unexpected meeting. For our nature-loving hearts, this means finding the liminal wherever rivers meet shorelines, waterfalls surge over craggy rocks, or California meets the Oregon state line that once separated us.

We covered over twenty thousand miles, not that it matters how far you go. It's all about how deep you dive.

Peter Jenkins

You will find symbols of thin places repeated in cultural art as classic shapes like the cross, the heart, and the concentric circle. You sense them in a dimly lit hospice room where only a spiritual veil separates life and death. You find them repeated in your dreams. I find a thin place in the state prison where inmates worship with a devotion not experienced in any church. A garden fragrant with sweet peas is a thin place for me, as is a desolate, wind-swept prairie. When I stand in either of these, I feel the impact of my two grandmothers.

"To seek such places is the vocation of the wise and the good," says Harvard professor and minister Peter Gomes, author of *The Good Book: Reading the Bible with Mind and Heart*.[4] On pilgrimage, seeking thin places is not just a way to enact faith

Stay-Safe Tips for Traveling Solo

- Stand tall, look confident, and walk strong. Project that you know where you're going.
- Fortify your mind with empowering thoughts.
- Don't go out alone after dark except in neighborhoods you know to be safe.
- Carry mace or a walking stick for stray dogs or potential attackers.
- Never give your contact information to a stranger. Become discerning; learn when *not* to give friendly people the benefit of the doubt.
- Carry your money in a belt tucked into your waistband, not in a purse, or even a backpack, that can be grabbed off your shoulder.
- Dress for the culture you're visiting, not your own culture. Look more gender neutral in certain cultures by tucking your hair up under a hat.
- Study your map before you go out. Memorize the names of streets you need to know.
- Keep snacks, magazines, and books in your room for entertainment on those evenings you spend with yourself. Light a candle, play music, take a bubble bath.
- If you are dining out alone and feeling uncomfortable with it, bring a book or newspaper to read. Practice enjoying *yourself*.
- Refuse to fuel fear. Do the safe thing, but don't let apprehension hold you back from enjoying the ride.

or find answers to your spiritual questions. Pilgrimage is to dare to ask—or simply to live the questions—and when we do so, we encounter liminal space.

As Sir Thomas Browne wrote in the seventeenth century, "We carry with us the wonders we seek without us."[5] Internal space is a thin place too. Therefore, I pack my soul's suitcase lightly, keeping preconceptions to a minimum. I tread lightly on the land, making as little impact as possible. In everything that happens to me, I try to remember, most of all, to be like the angels and take myself lightly. To be a pilgrim without spanning geography is to engage one's own inward adventures. Human experience everywhere shimmers with the dust of heaven.

131

Gutsy author and editor Marybeth Bond says we live our lives in one of three ways: as a saga, a treadmill, or a pilgrimage. How do you want to live? Let the quandaries lead you someplace. Through the passages of the thin places to which they take you, you become savvy, sensually enlightened, and spiritually sensitized.

"Charitable views of men and things cannot be acquired by vegetating in our little corner of the earth all one's lifetime," wrote humorist Mark Twain.[6] Understand what pilgrimage with all its adventures will give you. It will diminish stereotyping of others and encourage you to get real. It will open up possibilities for your future and offer new ways to think about old things. It will give you prestige among others and distinguish you in a crowd. It will give you something to talk about at parties! It will add to your life résumé and advance your credibility as a wise woman.

If our lives are dominated by a search for happiness, then perhaps few activities reveal as much about the dynamics of this quest—in all its ardor and paradoxes—than our travels.

Alain de Botton

Can we take a cue from the vagabonding movement that sprang up the 1960s and reached its heyday in the 1970s? It is being reinvented today. The idea of wandering packs negative connotations, linking back to the Hebrews' wilderness experience in Canaan. But can one wander with intention? Yes. Finding myself in the experience of pilgrimage, I've stopped asking, "Are we there yet?" If I hurry the process, I miss something. I miss the fact that the journey itself is the destination. I miss all the thin places along the way. I'm always on a journey anyway, because I'm never in the same place I left a minute ago.

Pilgrimage has been called a graduate program for the wild at heart. Scottish author Robert Lewis Stevenson said, "I travel

The Absolute Essentials

Heading out for a weekend or for several weeks? Either way, you'll want a bag of sample-size necessities easy to reach. Pack them in a ziplock bag so you see what you're looking for without rummaging around. Here is my list of twenty absolute essentials:

- your personal medications/vitamins
- pain reliever
- breath mints
- Band-Aids
- hazelnuts (for any kind of travel sickness)
- tampons
- mini flashlight
- tissues
- handiwipes
- duct tape
- eyedrops
- earplugs
- eyeshade
- one change of underwear
- fleece socks
- protein bar
- nail file and clippers
- folding scissors
- small stick stain remover
- ten one-dollar bills and a roll of quarters (pack in a snack-size ziplock bag)

not to go anywhere, but to go. . . . The great affair is to move."[7] When moving on a wild ride, the only rule is to hang on tight. Living a life on the edge, a life that has exposed me to the thin places, I've learned three things. First, I have learned in the most mundane of places to look deeply into what I see. Having done that, I always learn something new, something I needed to know in order to get to where I am going.

Second, I have learned that risk is inevitable anyway. Getting up in the morning is a risk. Going to bed and losing consciousness is a risk. And every forward movement in between puts me at risk. Therefore, I've made the decision to live until I die. I've made the decision to go ahead and explore new territory on my way through this life's reality.

Third, I've learned that every journey comes full circle. Absolutely everything belongs. Every experience counts—even heartbreak. Every mile, every threshold, brings me back where I started. Therefore, there is nothing to fear. My pilgrimages have been characterized by looking harder at what I thought was real, taking leaps of faith when I realized it wasn't, and expecting my pathway to circle around by a different route back home again. When I cross the threshold into what was familiar, I will never see it in quite the same light again.

> If a man set out from home on a journey and kept right on going, he would come back to his own front door.
>
> Sir John Mandeville

A threshold, defined as a physical demarcation such as a raised slab in a doorway preventing water from flowing into a house, separates one thing from another. It keeps the outside from getting inside. It keeps the inside from getting outside, at least without some notice. In Asia, these places are often guarded by statues of dogs or dragons. In our culture, statues or depictions of angels are often placed at the front door. Horseshoes, a symbol of plenty or good luck, are traditional in the western USA. For Orthodox Jews, the *mezuzah* is attached to the door. It is a parchment scroll inscribed with the words from Deuteronomy 6:4–9 and 11:13–21 and the name *el Shaddai*, "the Provider." All of these symbols of threshold denote protection and provision.

When I saw the two Haitian toddlers sitting on the threshold of their house surrounded by muddy green water, I knew this was a scene that would leave me changed. The place demanded to be noticed. To be given a second thought. A third thought. A fourth thought. I wanted to close up the gap, to prevent the mud and the ooze of life from getting into their home. I wanted to set the girls in a safe place where they might get more than a few grains of rice, where they might not suffer the flow of the world's curse of poverty. I wanted to reinforce the veil of the thin place, to sew it in comforting fabrics like the new comfy sofa throw I had just purchased at my favorite department store. To witness this was hard pilgrimage. But I was moving toward something. My pathway circles around past this place again and again. In my mind, this hut in Haiti is a place where human aspiration and human suffering meet in the light of eternity.

I seek these kinds of places; I am drawn to them. In *The Necessity of Experience*, Edward Reed writes, "The psychosocial ills that beset many of us today stem largely from the degradation of opportunities for primary experience. We become increasingly unable to function in the real world. We shelter in the pseudo- and virtual realities created for us by others and take our own paths less and less frequently."[8] And so I revisit myself. My fears. My agendas, hidden or not. My secret yearnings. Some of my quests may have to be abandoned. Places in my faith are sorely tried.

Like everyone else who has ever been on pilgrimage, I don't have to have a bigger purpose than to simply go and look. I am exposing myself to something bigger than I am. Something closer to the kingdom of heaven. It is changing me. I trust it will come full circle and change the world.

Unpacking Latin America

A Pilgrim's Profile: Vicki Kinney Petersen

How I learned that making a difference
will require emptying yourself into a
place and the breaking of all your
stereotypes

Our happiest moments as tourists seem to come when we stumble
upon one thing while in pursuit of something else.

Lawrence Block

Vicki Kinney arrived in San Jose, Costa Rica, with a mission. Her goal was to start a community like the one she'd been part of near Washington DC. Not intending to go there and get married, Vicki met the unexpected: the man of her dreams. An American working with World Vision International, Paul Petersen, became her husband by the end of seven months. As part of a nonprofit organization working toward development in over a hundred countries, Vicki says, "That's what took me all over the world."

When her husband wasn't opening up offices in new countries, requiring longer stays, he and Vicki traveled on assignment for six to twelve weeks living in Ethiopia, Cambodia, Thailand, and Kenya. Vicki says her family returned to the U.S. nearly twenty years ago for only one reason. They made a decision to live out the things they'd learned. "We saw how well people in those cultures take care of their elderly," Vicki says. "We respected this honoring of sages and elders. We wanted to respect our investment internationally and have it count for something."

Vicki, who is a life coach and women's workshop leader in Lakewood, Colorado, says, "The joy of travel is having your paradigms changed. Personal transformation is vital. That's the bottom line." Vicki says her first encounter overseas was seeing the difference between the haves and the have-nots. She'd heard Americans talk about worldwide poverty but then say, "We can't make a dent."

"Once overseas myself, I learned the opposite," Vicki says. "You walk beside people, and you enter into their story and their journey. By offering who you are and paying attention to someone else, you celebrate who they are and what they're about. In the process, you both are changed."

Vicki's lifelong mentor, an American woman named Mary McCormick, had lost her husband and, with seven children grown, left her home to devote herself to the poor in Colombia.

In a barrio outside Bogata, Vicki accompanied Mary on her mission several times a week. "We took the bus up the mountain until we had to walk," Vicki says. "Then on a massive hillside covered with cardboard shacks roped or nailed or wired together, we offered milk or food. We also tried to locate children who had no school supplies or uniforms, offering to buy them with money we'd collected from nonprofits.

"We'd see eight people crammed into a dirt-floor shanty where at night they all piled onto one mattress. The women cooked over a small fire in a hole by the door. I may have been one of the haves, but I saw that both those women and I had the same pumping heart. We had this flesh on these bones. We had the same mind that wanted to grow and learn and see our children thrive."

There was so much common ground, Vicki explains. "Seeing their simplicity and receiving their love was transforming me," she says. "Their brokenness and compassion for me began to change my whole worldview in every way."

Vicki often sensed a drastic conflict in ideology and custom between other cultures and her own. "I experienced how the families worship dead ancestors and call them forth to be a part of their lives. It bothered me. But I learned there's a way of honoring other people's history and story even when you don't agree with them. I've learned ways to creatively celebrate what can be celebrated in every culture. It's been my privilege to respect and learn everything I can from them. The customs of other cultures are part of a people's rootedness. I was always fascinated by how people's experience brings them to the place they are in life. Observation while traveling really breaks your own stereotypes."

Vicki struggled more often with women's silly superstitions. She tells about women coming to help with her housework and refusing to iron shirts on rainy days. "They believed that if it was raining, you'd have a spell put on you if you turned on anything hot. I just worked around that. I'd say. 'Give me that iron, I'll do it. It's not a big deal.'

"I was forever learning about things that limit people's ability to do what they want to do," Vicki says. But her most difficult struggle was with the Machista mentality of Latin America. "Male dominance," she says, "was not okay with me. I was put off that women were disempowered because they didn't have a voice. I was hurt and saddened, and I grieved. I wanted to make things different."

In fact, traveling among many different kinds of folks drove Vicki to want to be an agent of change wherever she went. "I learned to recognize needs," she says. "I discovered the power and opportunity I had as an educated person. I began to speak what I saw." Living five years in Costa Rica and nearly three in Colombia, Vicki says, "Making a difference will always take emptying yourself into a place and waiting until you're trusted. In Latin culture especially, you have to wait. It takes a long time for a foreigner to have a voice. Still, the poor are more trusting simply because they have little to lose. We can start there."

9

Mission Possible

Just Live It

We have to understand how to live out there, and what's required and what you can get away with, and what you can leave behind and what you can't leave behind and what makes humans continue to work together as a team because if they don't work together as a team, then you're not going to get your job done. And you can't just project the answer to that question, you have to go out there and live it to get the answer.

Colonel Susan J. Helms

One hundred years ago, few women dreamed of orbiting the earth in an international space station as Colonel Susan Helms did on the *Alpha*. But look; anything is possible. You may feel that the journey of your dreams is out of the question. But think about it. You can go anywhere you dream of going if you want to go badly enough. Start by finding out where you truly want to go. Are you motivated by beauty? Activity? The love of learning? Maybe you want to make a trip that will be a bonding experience with a daughter, mother, or friend. Maybe you just want to say you've been to some particular place because everyone else you know has been there. Or because no one else you know has been there!

Currently, I'm dreaming of the Cinque Terra in Italy. My girlfriend spent time there recently and fell in love with that hilly region where intimate villages are connected only by footpaths. When she offered to let me borrow the photographs she took, I didn't hesitate to accept. I know feasting my eyes on those blue coastal waters and the sand-colored buildings will trigger my imagination, the first step to going anywhere.

I'm propelled forward by the simple fact that to see is to believe, to visualize is to travel halfway there. Scientists say that the brain cannot differentiate between what is seen with physical eyes and what is imagined with the mind's eye. As a teenager, I didn't know that hanging a poster of the Swiss Matterhorn on my bedroom wall was the first step in actually going there in person, looking at it from the little village at its foot, which I did years later.

So let the dreaming begin! Imagine a place somewhere on the globe. Sit with the thought of it for a few minutes. Look it up in an encyclopedia or on the Internet. Buy a map, pick up a travel magazine, or rent a video about it at the library. Put up a poster—or a collage of photos from that place—in the kitchen. Then notice how what you dream about starts to materialize around you. Watch. You'll find newspaper clippings, see articles about it in magazines, or hear bits about it on TV. Listen to what experienced travelers say about the place you want to go. Listen to everything they don't say.

Wonder about what it would take to get to your ideal destination—without needing to know how right now. Allow questions to arise in you while waiting and thinking about it. Be a spy looking for hidden clues to places and culture and yourself. Be

Win the Hearts of Locals

Greet shop people with eye contact. There are things to beware of—in southern Italy, for example, women won't want to make eye contact on the street with passersby, particularly men. And in some places, beggars, especially children who beg, won't let you alone once you show that you've noticed them. Your spirit will make you discerning. Just be open to showing respect for people in general and validating their personhood.

Be classy, not crass with displays of affection. Remember that Europeans and people of many other cultures aren't as outgoing or casual about meeting strangers as Americans are. But there are other ways they may startle us. In Austria, for example, staring is not considered rude. In Denmark, you will be considered rude if you don't offer a handshake to people you meet. In many countries or states, public displays of affection are not appropriate. In others, everything is!

Ask questions about sights or the history of a place. When inquiring how to locate a particular sight, let curiosity lead you to more inventive questions that show appreciation for local color and customs.

Be thankful and grateful everywhere to everyone. Every individual, no matter the culture, deserves courtesy and respect. Make a game of offering it to others, especially when they don't offer it to you.

Take small, inexpensive, easy-to-carry gifts for potential hosts. You may meet people who invite you into their homes for a meal or for coffee. A box of pretty cards, a souvenir of your home state, or trinkets popular among young people are nice to bring. Children will be amused by American coins and love to receive pennies and nickels in small bundles tied with a tiny American flag. Teenagers love arm patches and necklaces of all kinds. I wear inexpensive versions of popular styles and when admired, remove them and hand them over. It makes you feel good all day.

Take photos of your house, family, and pets, along with postcards of your hometown to show people you meet along the way. Ask to take photos of their homes, pets, and family. It will make their day! When in France, I started asking people with French poodles—they were strolling everywhere—if I might take their photos. They were charmed by the idea, and my album of poodles now makes me smile because I remember the joy it brought.

PASSPORT

Ask passersby to take photographs of you in front of scenic places. Most will love to do so. Then tell them you want to take one of them too or ask another passerby to take your photo with them! You'll get a lot of silly and happy smiles.

a pirate looking for hidden treasure. Be a mystic looking for an epiphany. Be a wise woman following a star. And even before you set out, accept joy in your dreams of travel—proof of your own right to be alive and thriving on this earth.

What lies behind us and what lies before us are tiny matters compared to what lies within us.

Oliver Wendell Holmes

In the statement of the first female astronaut at the beginning of this chapter are the sacred questions we must ask of travel anywhere: What will be required out there? What should be left behind? What must not be left behind? What can we take away from unexpected situations? How can we work together with others along the way? On the open road—land, sea, or space—there are no perfect formulas.

Anxious thoughts may arise in you about the journey itself. Expect these. Let them simply be. But know that any negative idea or doubt is already doomed. It will be overpowered by your own positive energy and vision. If the steps you make to activate your dreams fall through, don't worry. There are often many roadblocks or delays before we get to where we want to go. Wait. Because you are most definitely on your way.

It doesn't take the training or the courage of an astronaut to live the impossible. Joy Broyles Yohay's dream trip started before she was grown. "I needed to test a childhood vision of myself that I was, at heart, an explorer. I had to do something bold—on my own and for myself." Yohay writes about her midlife, self-confrontational adventure: "Pulsating, riveting, difficult India was everything I wanted it to be."[1]

Did she say "difficult" India? So why should everything be easy? My personal motto or rule for travel has always been this:

I'm not going to sit home and wait as long as the world is turning. Risk will always be here. I won't be. Once, I spent a day sightseeing through London in drenching rain. The sky was losing what light it had given me as the sun set beyond the Thames River. As it did, the rain stopped falling. Before I returned to Essex, where I lived and worked, I decided to stop in at one of those small, charming British pubs. Beside the fire, I fell into conversation with a young man who worked on river barges. He invited me for a moonlit tour of the Thames to see the homes of movie stars and rock stars along its banks.

I probably should have been thinking, *Yeah, sure, fella; no way!* But I'd already made a decision to use the gift of fear to alert me to potential danger while living as a pilgrim on this earth. Fear is a friend when it gives you messages to wake up and watch out. Whether or not it was a good decision, I don't know. I can only say we jumped into his boat and took off under clear skies along the river, now studded with lights from the buildings and homes along its banks. That young man made no romantic move, or any other kind of move, toward me. What I remember was a spectacularly lovely evening that I was certain didn't happen to ordinary tourists locked in their hotel rooms.

Because of our own country's astounding crime rate, women traveling alone can be put off from adventure. In other cultures, however, crime is often less of a problem. The editors of *A Woman's World* say that polite and firm rejections of male advances are usually honored, or you can bring a stick and use it![2] I believe you learn as you travel. Listen to your conscience and the spirit within that moves you to the right place at the right time. Take caution when you feel the impulse that whispers of danger or warns you just to be wary. You may discern what to do in an instant. You may back away and take the safe route or move forward on a precarious way. Only you know what is right for you.

Photo Ops Galore

I always bring a camera with me on trips, but I end up taking dumb shots and not getting the ones I want. It's taken me a long time to learn how to find and shoot what I will later love to look at. Even if you don't have an expensive camera, disposable ones are not bad. Digital cameras, of course, allow you to send photos home right away or share with local people. However you do it, make good photos a good habit. Just shoot.

Take lots of photos of people and include plenty of yourself. Put yourself into scenarios. If you want to take shots of the cute red phone booths in London, get someone to snap you standing inside. A booth full of sunflowers at the Salzburg open-air market? Step into the middle of them and smile.

Take fewer photos of famous sights where you can buy postcards. But always capture special situations: that glowing backlight on the Eiffel Tower or the sun setting over Tenerife. People in the photos will give a sense of size as well as add the human element and emotional appeal.

Be conscious of composition. Shoot from different angles, look for interesting arrangements of shapes, notice any distracting background behind the subject you're shooting and avoid it if possible. Look for ways to enhance the simplicity of your shot.

In some cultures, photographing is still taboo, so always ask before you shoot a photo. Some people will say yes and then insist on money afterward, so be forewarned, and carry dollar bills to hand out just in case.

Children love to have their photos taken and will ham it up for the camera. You'll get your best shots of their diverse and loveable faces. I found that wearing a Mickey Mouse watch playing a Disney theme song gathered kids and served as an icebreaker to get their photos.

Take photos of details and get close to objects of interest. The face of a gargoyle, for example, is more interesting than a photo of the entire cathedral. The pattern of colorful stucco in Greece or the lines of a weathered face are more intriguing than a shot of a crowd in the village.

To travel is to possess the world.

Burton Holmes

I love daring things, but I won't climb a mountain that I have to rope up for. I won't kayak on a class five river. I won't shoot the half-pipe while snowboarding. Those are my current rules, but even those are open to change, depending on my physical condition, the presence of a quality guide, and my own slow-growing daredevil factor. "If there be anywhere on earth a lover of God who is always kept safe, I know nothing of it, for it was not shown to me," wrote English anchoress Julian of Norwich. "But this was shown: that in falling and rising again we are always kept in that same precious love."[3]

I am ready to accept inconvenience, renew faith in myself at every turn, and make room for the extraordinary. I am always looking for the value-added quality in every place I visit. I want the patina of place that communicates what is authentic here and why it is good I am here at all.

A pilgrim will embrace new ways and customs wherever she goes. She'll interpret things that happen with a willingness to at least try to understand. She creates her own experience from her unique perspective. She draws on personal sensibilities to find her path, the one nobody else knows about. The fringe benefit is discovering and uncovering things regular folks don't see. The editors of *A Woman Alone* tell us that "with each misadventure and triumph, we learn that the world reveals itself in startling and vivid ways."[4]

When my friend, Chip, a secular Franciscan, visited Assisi, Italy, the home of St. Francis, the church there was closed and locked. Disappointed but not disarmed, he circled around the back of the property and found another door, slightly ajar. Not at all shy, he followed steps down to a smaller chapel, then another set of steps leading to a crypt where, according to tradition, St. Francis was buried. Around it, an Italian church choir gathered, singing in Latin. Chip's curiosity was rewarded by a profound worship experience that was the highlight of his pilgrimage. When you travel anywhere, he says, always pack a lot of spunk and a little bit of sass.

Allah has laid out the earth for you like a vast carpet so that you will travel its endless roads.

The Koran

Seeking to stay on the growing edge, I've learned not to mind being rebuffed in the process of exploration. Once, wanting a photograph of myself with one of those fairy-tale guards in the black furry hats at Buckingham Palace, I sauntered up beside one of them, instructing my sister to snap a picture. Suddenly, the guard became extremely angry, communicating that he was off limits. I honestly had no idea that was not allowed. I was sorry I had broken the rules, and I have the darling photo to prove it!

An adventuress celebrates differences in culture, customs, and language, even when she makes a mistake or when the joke is on her. While an ordinary tourist is observing art and artifacts, a pilgrim is observing lifestyles and cultural personality. I once was soundly scolded for leafing through a magazine off the newsstand in Denmark, something quite acceptable in our own country. The fact that browsing through a magazine before buying it was not in the least allowable in the Danish culture was far more interesting than the magazine itself. The verbal beating was worth it. After all, Henry David Thoreau got it right when he commented, "It's not worth the while to go round the world to count the cats in Zanzibar."[5]

If you're comparing everything you see with something at home, and judging it thereby, why go at all? Believe it or not, the first time I traveled in Europe as a twenty-one-year-old, I ridiculously compared everything I saw to Disneyland. Finding myself in a land of tiny kingdoms, all of them oozing charm, tapped into a childhood wonder I'd known only through Disney productions. So what? A person always works within a framework of emotional responses developed over a lifetime. Be easy on yourself. Be forgiving of yourself. When on the road, take mistakes and rebuffs in stride. Your own attitude is intrinsic to the value of your trip.

Traveling by car through Poland (when it was still behind the Iron Curtain) with four others, we were stopped by the police, who took our passports and then demanded over two hundred dollars for a trumped-up traffic violation. Arguing did not help as more police were called who threatened to impound our van. A half ton of Christian literature and Bibles was hidden in secret compartments throughout the vehicle, built for such missions. Had the van been searched, we'd have found ourselves in a Polish prison. We quickly gathered all the cash we had between the five of us, handed it over, and let the policeman know that's all we had. Soon we were on our way. Mistake or not, sometimes you take your lumps and leave well enough alone.

I call them true pilgrims traveling towards the bliss of heaven . . . to know truly and keep faithfully the biddings of God.

William Thorpe

Spain's Teresa of Avila led a Catholic-reform movement in the sixteenth century, establishing and linking convents throughout the country. Texts say she "traveled tirelessly in all weathers, braving thieves and rat-infested inns." In fact, she was once described

Prayer Journal

The people you meet will become the most important part of any trip. You never know who they will be or when they will show up or how they will affect your life. But looking back, you'll want to remember. And in many cases, you'll be moved to pray for certain people or certain needs once you get back home.

Glue photos of people you want to pray for in your journal. Note their names if you have them or brief descriptions that will later jog your memory. What distinguished their appearance? Tall and thin, bright eyes, big hands? Do you remember what made them light up or what burden they carried?

The things that are important to you will be the things that are most important to people all over the world: love of family; the future of their children; the health of our planet and our political systems; health, love, and energy for our various callings on this earth. We all want something to give the world.

Write down Scriptures that come to mind as you pray, along with quotes or shards of poetry that come to mind. Write a prayer beside the photo or description. When you pick up your prayer journal, notice which memories keep coming to mind and whose faces capture your attention that day. Just looking at the photos and remembering is itself a kind of prayer.

by a papal delegation from Rome as "a restless gadabout, a disobedient, stubborn, ambitious woman." But history tells us that her wit and humor remained intact. Once, when tossed from a carriage, she exclaimed, "Lord, if this is how you treat your friends, no wonder you have so few!" Despite her frail health and the resistance to the reform she worked for, she continued to travel until age sixty.[6]

A phrase I once read applies to people like Teresa of Avila: "It is not the stars that create light, but light that creates the stars."[7] We who walk this earth are not put here to do good works; it is the Good Work who, in us, walks the earth. We simply live out the light and purpose of our source. Being nominated as a gadabout is a beautiful compliment for adventurers who spread light upon the pathway of a dark world. Let your feet follow your heart. Isn't this how the saints walked on this planet?

My daughter once asked me, "Mommy, when you were a little girl, what did you want to be when you grew up?" When I told her I wanted to be a missionary, she literally fell off her chair laughing. (I wondered what was so funny!) At the time, I was disappointed I'd not fulfilled that dream. Or had I? Living abroad for more than fourteen years of my adult life, the spirit of exploration was at work in me. A desire to travel, to move along, to experience new places was always with me. The mission I was called to is simply to open my eyes. Perhaps to be a missionary is as much to be changed by a place or a people group as it is to change one or the other.

At the Western Wall in Jerusalem, I scribbled a request for a certain issue onto a small piece of paper and wedged it in a crevice in the ancient stones, along with many others, withering there for years. Perhaps it was the most profound thing I have done in all my travels. To be a pilgrim on this earth is to participate in the holy. It doesn't mean that every experience you have will bring an epiphany, render a spiritual insight, or bring someone to the kingdom of God. To participate in the holy is simply to take joy in the world, and in so doing to offer a smile, a piece of bread, or a prayer.

Part 4

The Adventure
Is Already within You

10

Travel Alchemy

It Changes You

There is only one journey. Going inside yourself.

Rainer Maria Rilke

Travel is a mirror that reveals to you the best things about yourself. Redefining your identity as you travel is absolutely life affirming, and one of adventure's best rewards. You get to try on different hats—and smiles. You get to experiment with your life through different approaches to people and tradition. "A mind once stretched by a new idea can never go back to its original dimensions," said Oliver Wendell Holmes.[1] That is exactly why one of the best things about travel is that it changes you.

Fortunate are those pilgrims who know that travel is biased on the side of personal renewal. My definition of successful travel is anything that makes me grow and transcend the limitations of my own mind and mundane habits. Whether going abroad or around the block, honoring the changes in ourselves is the key to successful travel. By it we participate in the opportunity of "recalibrating our spirits to the mystery that is all around us."[2]

When my middle daughter, Leyah, flew home for Christmas in 2001, three months after the hijackings of September 11, she left from the Boston airport. I thought she would be nervous—I was. Leyah called me from the airport just before departure and cheerfully said, "If anything happens to me, don't worry; I've had a good life! I've gotten to do everything I wanted to do!" Here was a kid who could arrive in Paris by herself and during a three-hour layover see the Louvre, go shopping, lunch at a sidewalk café, and be back for her connecting flight. Here was a kid who had jogged along the chaotic streets of Port au Prince, Haiti, wandered through Harlem at night, sashayed around isolated Prudence Island. Flying in for the holidays under a nationwide orange "terror alert" didn't worry her. At nineteen years old she had already found that traveling—anywhere—is worth the risk if it gets you where you want to go.

There is a gypsy hiding in my own soul, and that can't be all bad. I must admit, however, that the night before each departure of my own, I start feeling nervous. I say to myself, *I don't want to go. I wish I hadn't decided to do this. I wish I were just staying home.* This happens every time I'm going to leave—no kidding! I wrestle with the doubt and finally accept it as part of the territory. Dame Freya Stark, who traveled in the Middle East on her own, noted that we do best to accept what comes: "You have no idea what is in store for you, but you will, if you are wise and know the art of travel."[3] At the end of every trip or the end of life itself, you'll say, "I've had a good life; I've gotten to do what I wanted to do."

Listening Is a Trip

When traveling throws you into contact with lots of different kinds of people (and it will), one of the best things you can pack is a strong set of listening skills. When you listen, you are put into a gifted role—one that allows you to use great imagination. Remember:

- Listening does not mean checking out of conversation. In fact, it's the opposite. It requires your active participation. A good listener understands that the beautiful answer to any human dilemma is always a more beautiful question.
- When listening, make eye contact. Send positive thoughts, even feelings, through your own eyes. Notice the tone and character of the other person's voice. Allow it to offer you messages.
- Listen to everything unsaid, left out—and seek to understand why that might be important. Reflect back thoughts in a word or two, giving encouragement to amplify, correct, or clarify what was said.
- Listen with affection; show that you are feeling "tell me more." Look for what makes eyes twinkle or light up and causes a smile to erupt. Look for luminance and keep listening until you see it.

The listening process is redemptive. It changes perspectives, feelings, attitudes, and even circumstances without you saying a word, because being artfully listened to changes people. Not only will you learn a lot, you'll offer validation, hope, respect, and honor. The world will become a better place to be. Listen deeply to everyone you meet and you'll discover it's a sacred thing. You may be holding a cracked heart or a chipped dream that simply needs to be healed by empathy and a quiet spirit.

I think when you are truly stuck, when you have stood still in the same spot for too long, you throw a grenade in exactly the spot you were standing in, and jump, and pray. It is the momentum of last resort.

Renata Adler

By going someplace—anyplace—adventurers act as magnets, attracting experiences to inspire, challenge, and renovate stagnant or staid minds. Once, I boarded a plane to Tel Aviv. I was just coming out of my divorce, and the trip seemed like a getaway gift, until I got on the plane. As we took off, an emotional pin shook loose. To my embarrassment, I began to cry, fighting to regain composure. With the grace of an angel, the man sitting just across the aisle started talking to me at just that moment. As if he hadn't noticed my struggle, he told me how, as an Israeli living in the States, he was returning to visit his family. In the process, he rescued me from humiliation and overwhelming feelings that had nothing to do with the trip. I have learned to trust the process of being renewed on the move, because travel is kingdom work.

Breaking new ground to learn these truths is never easy, of course. "There is something inherently unsettling yet wonderfully exciting about picking up two suitcases and leaving behind all the comforts in your life," writes Shelly Hawkins of her first time abroad as a student. "I learned that my strength reveals itself when I encounter new challenging situations. I learned that I really could go for three months without my curling iron. I learned that I love the English fog when it hangs low over vast green fields of grass. I learned that my heart had foreign signatures on it. Yet encountering all of this took me by surprise."[4]

The secret of going anywhere is to show up for yourself first of all. You have started on the path; you are already going somewhere. The joy is not only planning what you want to enjoy along the way but enjoying the process of seeing your plan happen—or not! Truth is, the adventure is not only within you; you are the adventure. The real place you are going to visit is within yourself. Everything else is peripheral. Even if you travel where everyone else has gone before, your experience of it will be like that of no one else.

What the pilgrims see along the way depends on what they are capable of seeing.

Anne Armbrecht Forbes

We're all on a journey. Frank MacEowen exhorts you to "become your own mapmaker on the path of your life."[5] Your questions act as a compass for the journey. Where would you go if you could go anywhere and do anything you wanted to do there? If there was nothing holding you back? What do you want to learn about life? Where might you go to receive those lessons? What makes you feel energized? How much do you want it? What are you willing to sacrifice to go get it? When will you know you're there? Who will inspire you to keep going?

To travel is to engage the power to amaze yourself by being your own muse. St. Augustine regarded the world as a book: "Those who do not travel read only a page," he said. So wait no more to rock your world. Live impossibly passionately. Put on your traveling shoes and head over the rainbow, not over the hill. What did Jesus say about travel? Take the high road! For, he warned, the blind lead the blind, and both fall into a ditch. "Follow Me, and let the dead bury their own dead," he told the disciples.[6] So they did, and guess what? Their obedience was followed by a storm at sea. God never promised an easy way. He asked merely for us to do it anyway. Sending his friends out to travel, Jesus offered these words: "Freely you have received, freely give." And he advised them to be "wise as serpents and harmless as doves."[7]

These are beautiful words with which to embark on any journey. Write them in your travel diary. Send them to friends in a bon voyage card. Inscribe them on your soul. When you stumble along the way, remember that your face will be marred by sweat and dust, but you're a winner by virtue of the fact that you started out at all. I encourage you to embark upon your inner adventure at once so that when, unexpectedly, a window—or a cat door—opens for geographical pilgrimage, you are ready to pass through to your dream.

What and How to Pack

CARRY WITH YOU:

- Your driver's license and passport—and keep these on you, along with your wallet.
- A refillable bottle of water (collapsible canteens in sports backpacks are fantastic).
- Glasses and a neck chain for them or a small case that fits in a pocket.
- An extra layer in a natural fiber (cotton, silk, or wool blend), as airplanes can be hot or cold, regardless of the weather, and blankets may be in short supply. Choose something inexpensive and simple to slip on or off.
- Backup cash in tens and twenties hidden in a money belt and the same amount hidden in another place—a deep pocket in your cargo pants or a pin-on fabric envelope you tuck into a sock. Copy the numbers of your credit card and traveler's checks to leave with someone at home.
- Choose one great accessory that will accent your travel wardrobe. A really great scarf is light but colorful and keeps away drafts. One basic but fabulous piece of jewelry can offer a feeling of being dressed up without overdoing it.
- Wear one great pair of leather shoes (sandals that strap around your heel in summer; hiking shoes or boots in winter).

PACK IN YOUR CARRY-ON:

- A fiber-rich snack. Bring your favorite trail mix, protein bar, whole wheat crackers, dried fruit, juice box, turkey or beef jerky.
- A must-read book you've been putting off reading. This is the time to do it—finally!
- A walkman and extra batteries, plus your favorite CDs.

We could never learn to be brave and patient if there were only joy in the world.

Helen Keller

James Joyce wrote, "Sometimes the longest way round is the shortest way home."[8] What he meant, I think, is that sometimes

- Specialty tea bags (Good Earth/Constant Comment/green or herbal tea) as an alternative to coffee onboard.
- Body lotion or oil and lip balm to moisturize; those flights really dry the skin.
- Sturdy sunglasses and sunscreen for when you arrive.
- Basic makeup kit (keep it simple): lip color, combo foundation/powder compact, smudge-proof mascara, and one or two pieces that make you feel stunning (blush or shimmery lip gloss).
- A collapsible umbrella if going to a predictably rainy climate.
- Toiletries in small sizes: toothbrush and toothpaste, soap, makeup remover pads, lotion, deodorant, shower cap, razor, shampoo and conditioner, hair spray.

PACK IN YOUR SUITCASE FOR UP TO THREE WEEKS OF SIGHTSEEING:

- Three pairs socks in different weights—for warmth, for hiking, for comfort.
- One dress in lightweight natural fibers.
- One pair cargo pants or khakis with lots of pockets.
- One pair jeans.
- One pair easy-drying sweats.
- One shorter skirt.
- One longer skirt.
- One pair leggings or cotton shorts and T-shirt for sleeping.
- One or two sleeveless tops in summer.
- One or two short-sleeve knit tops.
- One or two long-sleeve knit tops easy to wash and fast to dry (a collapsible hanger is handy).
- One light jacket.
- One warm but lightweight sweater.
- Three or four pairs easy-dry underwear and a vial of hand soap for washing.

shortcuts just won't do. Sometimes the longer, harder way is the shorter way after all. I relive a scary experience as a young woman in a country that took me totally by surprise at every turn. I am twenty-three again and trying to take shortcuts through Jerusalem's labyrinth of old streets, alleyways, and tunnels—dark and crowded. I want to find that shop with dresses that are hand embroidered by Arab women. The more I search, the more I get lost. The stench of sheep entrails pervades the corridor as women bustle about from the vegetable booth to the butcher shop—yes, they really do buy those chicken feet and lamb heads hanging in the window!

I'm invited into a carpet shop for tea, along with a Coptic priest, by an older Arab shopkeeper. I ask about the embroidery shop. Not much English spoken here. I know it is growing dark outside, so I decline the tea; I don't want to walk back to my house after nightfall. The new city will be bustling with traffic. But here, lost in Jerusalem's old city, I start to panic. *Okay,* I decide. *Forget the black linen dress with the multicolored threads stitched in a geometric pattern you saw last week. Just find the way out.*

Stop, Marlee, I tell myself in another, calmer voice. *Close your eyes. Release your fear. Walk slowly. Don't look for shortcuts. Take the long way. Take the winding way that goes farther back before it twists up and out toward the Jaffa Gate.*

Heading home once more, I pass the Garden Tomb, known as Gordon's Calvary. The last tourists are leaving in the twilight. The last buses are leaving the bus station across the street. I walk down Street of the Prophets, getting closer to the hostel. I notice a man following me. A tall, spindly man. Young. Not menacing looking. But definitely keeping pace with me when I speed up or slow down. I dodge into a bookstore. He follows. I turn around the shelves in the middle of the store and head out again, then start to run home. *Will the buzzer gate at the hostel open when I get to the fence? Will anyone be inside to push the button and let me in right away?* I pray hard. Harder.

I round the corner running as the man jogs after me. At the gate, something unusual has happened. It has been left open! I run in and slam it behind me. "Oh, blessed Virgin Mary!" I cry, hoping that doesn't sound like blasphemy, hoping God is okay with that. For the next week, I don't go out alone.

With Yourself or By Yourself?

> You need a clear feeling for your own boundaries. . . . The more
> you become sure of your own center, the more you can also open
> your boundaries. Otherwise, you'll spend your whole life
> defending those boundaries.
>
> Richard Rohr

Wondering how to make being alone work for you, not against you?
Keep these tips in mind:

- Refuse to be timid.
- Expose yourself to nuances of experience, not the same black and white.
- Work with your fears and let them serve you, not intimidate you.
- Opt to stay in small hotels or hostels where you meet people.
- Look for places with a common meeting area for evenings or breakfasts.
- Stay active doing things you love: Antique shopping? Art galleries?
- Eat well for vitality. Avoid blood-sugar drops by drinking unsweetened juice or munching on almonds, hazelnuts, walnuts, or soy nuts.
- Do at least one thing every day that stretches you: Eating out alone? Walking, instead of riding, to your destination?
- Keep a journal and colored pens in your bag. Make it craftsy. Use a small pair of folding scissors to snip photos from brochures and tickets, and include a small glue stick.
- Dress for the cultural climate you're in, but add a dash of your own style.
- Keep 9-1-1 on speed dial on your cell phone.
- If assaulted, yell, run. Don't allow yourself to be taken to a second location. Don't be compliant.
- If somebody gets too friendly, speak loudly and firmly. Ask them in a voice of authority to leave you alone; tell them you will call the police.
- Don't wear earphones or listen to music when you walk alone or jog. Use your ears, as well as your eyes, for safety. Don't be complacent.
- Choose a close-fitting purse with a sturdy strap and wear it under a jacket if possible. Walk with your hand on top of the flap or zipper.
- Have an understanding of the culture before you go so you at least know what is expected of you.
- Enjoy the fact that you can do what you want to do when you want to do it and stay open to spontaneity and serendipity. Go with the flow. Stay in the moment.
- Remember, you always have yourself, God, and the angels. You are never alone. You are not by yourself. You are with yourself. People can see the difference.

Travel will open you up to wonder and prayer and grace. It will use all of your senses. That's because when you are in a strange place, all your perceptions are heightened. No matter how frightening, when you're settled at home again, you'll wish for that time again. Are you trying to outrun trouble, like I did, running for your life through the busy streets? Of course, there are times when we all do this. But if you try to stay out of trouble, that's worse. You calcify. You end up closing yourself into your four walls, pulling the blinds. Shutting yourself behind closed doors.

Macon gazed out the cab window, considering the notion in his mind. He felt a kind of inner rush, a racing forward. The real adventure, he thought, is the flow of time; it's as much adventure as anyone could wish.

Anne Tyler Modarressi

Courage, said Ernest Hemingway, is "grace under pressure."[9] How many times will you find yourself under pressure when you go on pilgrimage? Plenty. But pressure is not a bad thing. Neither is rain, sleet, or snow. Neither is running out of money or having your passport stolen or losing your way. These are nothing more than the long ways around to grace. We seek good fortune, not realizing that we already are good fortune, as Walt Whitman pointed out. God's grace and our courage open ways for bad things to happen in order to see them being worked together for good. Certain odd things will occur when you have courage that never would have happened without it. Serendipitous things. Things that can never be forgotten. But this is what pilgrimage and adventure are all about.

I think my courage is becoming crusty the older I get. I used to be afraid of nothing. Now I am less flexible. Does our resilience grow rigid along with the pupils of our eyes after age fifty? An optometrist once explained to me that I can either go ahead and get glasses, needing stronger magnification all the time, or I can exercise my eyes by focusing hard without glasses and put off the inevitable a while longer. I think courage is the same way. I can take it out into the world, around the globe, and exercise it, or I can just stay home and ask, *Why should I go when I just don't have the verve I had when I was younger?*

I decide to fight the loss of courage just like I fight the loss of muscle tone by exercising regularly. I will do adventure for the timeless me, neither young nor old. This Marlee is saying, *Go, girl. Don't hold back anything from life. Be brave. You've not yet written your fill of stories.*

Go now, she tells me, *before you crust over entirely. Don't let me down. Take a path, any path, and follow it. Let your juicy, wise woman run with the surf or swing from a star. Your grandchildren will remember the twinkle in your eye. Your daughters will see aging not only with grace but also with gusto.*

Stop, Marlee, she says. *Close your eyes. Release your fear. Walk slowly. Don't look for shortcuts. Take the long way. Take the winding way that goes farther back before it twists up and out toward the Jaffa Gate.*

Big risks, "seeking out places where nobody else goes," model and entrepreneur Lauren Hutton says, make life worth living. She should know—she's been doing it for the last forty years, spending six months of each year on the road.

"The great thing about dangerous situations is that you are so alive," Hutton says. "You're learning. You're totally aware and you're fantastically young. You're five again. Everything is brand new. Simply traveling does that."[10]

When you bother to do the extraordinary, some rain will fall. Your capacity to deal with the unexpected will stretch. Wherever the extraordinary takes you, remember that there is no bad weather in life; it all belongs. But you can be inappropriately dressed for the weather. Courage is to be fully dressed for whatever happens. Aside from love, hope, and faith, travel is the greatest adventure in life. Ursula LeGuin put it succinctly: "It is good to have an end to journey toward, but it is the journey that matters in the end."[11]

Unpacking Vietnam

A Pilgrim's Profile: Linda Hays

How I learned that people the world over
are more alike than different

All God's children wear traveling shoes.

Maja Angelou

Images of Vietnam on TV when I was growing up in the 1960s
was all I knew of that country," says Linda Hays of her most
memorable trip. "When I visited there in 2003, I had no idea
what I was going to face. Would my husband and I be accepted as
Americans? Would we be safe? Would the food make us sick?"

Calling herself a worry wart, Linda, of Silverton, Oregon,
admits that her apprehension may have gone a bit overboard.
After all, she had traveled internationally before, visiting Uzbeki-
stan and Honduras in previous years. Linda, who is employed
by Hospice, also says, "I've learned that as a Christian I connect

with people of other religions because we share this world and we are more alike than different." In her research for this third trip abroad, she read that the people were remarkably gracious and the land beautiful. Her visit would be in conjunction with Northwest Medical Teams and Project Vietnam, an effort of the American Academy of Pediatrics. On this occasion, as one of more than 150 volunteers, Linda's task was to document the trip through photography. Her husband, a paramedic and contractor/builder would offer paramedic training as he does all over the world, donating his vacation time annually.

When the Hayses married in 1997, Linda was drawn into her husband's enthusiasm for Third World countries. "It came about that I was able to join him on the trips, and that was a turning point for me," Linda says. "I realized I can also do the kinds of things required by the sometimes primitive traveling conditions.

"In spite of my fears," Linda says, "once we got to Vietnam I was fascinated. I felt surprisingly in tune with the culture—and totally comfortable. The countryside and culture impressed me with its simplicity of lifestyle. All my apprehension melted away—except for traffic," Linda adds quickly. "You'd have to experience it!" She explains that Vietnam is literally "driven" by motorbikes. "Vehicles are whizzing all over," she says, "so trying to cross the street as a pedestrian, you just step out in the middle of them and hope to get to the other side. If you try to dodge them, you'll be in trouble."

Linda tells how one of the American team members was standing on a street corner looking for a break in traffic. After waiting an inordinately long time, an elderly Vietnamese lady came along, grabbed him by the arm, and got him safely across. "We laughed," she said, "at the upset of the classical stereotype of young men helping elderly ladies across the street."

Linda admits now that she will go anywhere in the world next time, even on her own. "You find out that people are people wherever you are." Once, touring a Vietnamese hospital through a labyrinth of buildings, Linda stopped to take some photos, then turned around and saw her group was gone. "I had no idea what happened," she explains. "No one spoke English. I could have wandered for hours looking for my group. I thought, *Just remember your wilderness training. Stay put.* So I stayed in the reception area, but people kept looking at me as if I wasn't supposed to be there." Later, a Vietnamese lady came up, took Linda's arm, and led her across the compound to be reunited with her group.

"I said later to my husband, 'Thanks for sending the cavalry!' But he hadn't even realized I was lost," she says. "That lady had just figured out I needed help. That kind of thing happens when you go overseas. People everywhere care for their children and families and other people. You learn that you also will be cared for. Friends say to me, 'Aren't you afraid to travel in those countries?' I answer, 'Well, upsetting things could happen here too. There are no guarantees. I finally got the message that life is to live and enjoy. I want to take full breaths of it, not sit around and worry. Why not experience what you can?

"If all we know of other cultures is what we see on TV," Linda says, "we begin to distrust them, because generally, it's all bad news. We all should travel everywhere so we can figure out that everyone in every culture is really okay." Linda found time to walk around Saigon, now called Ho Chi Minh City, with another female member of the team. "We jumped into cyclos, little bicycle carts like rickshaws, and my driver starts off heading right toward a huge bus. I scream. He yells, 'No trouble!' and suddenly the bus zooms right by me."

Later, Linda and her friend found the Vietnamese fast food venue called "No Noodles." She notes that Vietnam also has fabulous French cooking and delicious éclairs. But there is a certain kind of fruit, a delicacy, that is spiked like a little porcupine. "When you cut it open, it smells like rotting flesh," Linda says. In fact, she explains that in some hotels it is illegal to open this fruit in your room. "I never got to try it," she says. "Now I think, *Darn, I missed out*." She notes, "If you don't try everything, you'll regret it."

Inspired by the hardworking, entrepreneurial Vietnamese people, Linda enjoyed their creative flair whether observing a wedding party, noticing the unusual designs and cuts of clothing, or browsing artistic shop displays. "The Vietnamese are innovative builders too," she says. "They pay taxes only on the amount of ground space a building occupies, so their houses are tall and skinny.

"I feel an affinity to the way the Vietnamese culture closely examines things," Linda says. "We are connected regardless of tradition, language, or religion. I've learned that everything's up for grabs when you travel, and you have to be prepared to take things as they are. But when you do, you grow—in faith and love—the kind of love God has for all the people of the earth."

Why women should travel? "Because life is too short," Linda says. "Our lives are not a written script. Go for it. And take deep breaths."

11

Furious Faith in Forward Motion

Beyond the Mundane

Wherever you go, there you are.

Carl Franz

Apopular website noted that the average person spends 96,400 hours of his or her lifetime working. With all that concentration, doesn't everyone deserve a little time to recreate? For an average lifespan of seventy-five years, the time we are not working leaves 219,000 hours for sleeping and a remnant of 88,000 hours for other things. If the average person takes four weeks of vacation a year, that's 43,680 hours of vacation in a lifetime. What are you going to do with those nearly 50,000 hours—and even more if you count the retirement years after age sixty-five?

"I am the door," Jesus said of his place in people's lives. Then he refers to a going "in and out" to find pasture. Of his sheep he adds, "I have come that they may have life, and that they may have it more abundantly."[1] In evangelical terms, salvation is an issue of our eternal destiny, and Jesus is the threshold. In a broad sense, salvation is a matter of God actually inviting us to explore life by passing over that threshold on a regular basis in order to experience it abundantly.

This exploration is a great adventure in whatever form it takes. It includes our life work, doing what we are gifted for to bless the world. It includes time off to reinvent our inner resources, rejuvenate our inner lives, rebuild our grace. The idea of vacations, based on the original "holy days" of the church, means to vacate your residence, implying a change of location and routine. Vacations are where people sanctify their workaday lives, engage in physical activities that are fun or challenging, traverse a landscape they're not used to. What will you do with your forty-some-thousand hours of vacation? Will it be meaningful, pleasurable, and inspirational too?

We are transients, each in transition, on the way to our ultimate home, and so we trek on.

Jane Rubietta

There are lots of ways to get creative about annual vacations. It does not have to mean sightseeing, sunbathing, or sitting until everyone gets weary of the question, Are we there yet? Active adventure travel is big for women: river rafting, fly fishing, mountain climbing, and other risky exploits. The question is not, What's possible? but, What's popular? For the more sedate among us, or those for whom it's important to catch up on people missed amid busy workaday lives, we'll go for the gusto of girlfriends. In fact, girlfriend getaways are the new hot phenomenon that's sweeping the nation. In getaways together,

Five Big Travel Mistakes to Avoid

Rigid planning. Allow white space in your schedule. If you try to pack in too many events or destinations or too much sightseeing in one day, you'll end up disappointed and frazzled. There will be unexpected things that require your attention or beckon with a sense of serendipity. You'll meet people you want to spend time with, see places you want to go back to, experience delays, take care of personal business, take naps, wind down. Let your experience be what it is. Don't try too hard. Enjoy!

Overpacking. The old adage is true: Pack your bag, but then open it up and take out half of what you packed. Be severe. Think hard about the things you think you just have to have along. Delete half of them. Imagine yourself hauling your baggage from place to place where airport shuttles don't exist and bellhops aren't available. Go minimal. Go sleek. Pare down. You'll be so glad you did.

PASSPORT

Failure to laugh. Pack your sense of humor and don't lose it for anything! Practice looking at the funny side of things. Turn calamities upside down. Cast a different light on things that go wrong. You can handle a lot more than you think you can. You will always find a way to cope with difficulty. Stay calm in tight places. Take several deep breaths. Now laugh. Right out loud.

Carelessness with valuables. When push comes to shove in traveling mode, an attitude of meticulous care is indispensable. Take the extra moment to put the change from your purchase into your wallet before you leave the salesperson. Always replace your driver's license and passport immediately in that easy-to-reach designated place. Don't allow yourself to stuff it as you walk away and pick up a conversation with someone. Notice when strangers bump into you or are in contact with your person in crowded places. Never lay your valuables on a bedside table at night, even in a locked hotel room. Put them in a place where someone would have to dig for them in a suitcase or, better yet, under your pillow. Think about your valuables several times a day and recheck their location.

Lack of spirit (not lack of money). One thing is for certain: you'll always wish you'd brought more money. But how full are your reserves of positive attitude, optimism, sense of adventure, and spiritual energy? How full are your cisterns of grace for other people's faults and irritating quirks or the ability to accept what is?

Use a little time each day before you leave to read inspirational material and pray for the people you'll be traveling with and the people you'll be meeting.

sisters, girlfriends, and moms and daughters are enjoying the abundant life of mutual support in a context of entertaining community.

What do girlfriend getaways look like? They come in all shapes, sizes, and colors. Get together for coffee once a week or splurge on an entire week together at a beach cottage. Choose a long weekend in the spring for a break in the mountains or just a Saturday morning of antique sale-ing. Gather for brunch in someone's home or a favorite café. My friend Abby gets away with her mother and sisters each year while her two sons vacation with their dad. The girls head out somewhere different each year: shopping in Seattle's rambling downtown or renting a country villa in Italy (at a surprisingly low rate). But Abby's favorite place is the family lake house in Minnesota, where the girls just put up their feet and let their hair down.

A getaway takes a bit of spunk to pull together, especially if you're coming from different parts of the country. But if you've got more than one willing heart, you can delegate the details. Experts say that, like a wedding, the key is not to get bogged down in the planning. The most important tools for making a girlfriend getaway happen are flexibility and the desire to reconnect. What most of us want is to see each other, laugh together, and have plenty of time to talk in a relaxing environment. Sightseeing is optional. You are the entertainment!

Bring only ultracomfy clothes; there's no trying to impress one another on a girlfriend getaway. Bring your CDs (make certain someone brings a player) and snacks to share, elaborate or not. It'll create ambience if everyone brings something special for each person. It can be as simple as a quote or Scripture for each person on a pretty homemade card, a gag gift, a panty exchange, or even a recipe. Bring manicure essentials and an assortment of fingernail polishes. Games like Cowgirls or Chicken Soup for the Soul are terrific for a gang of women who want to let their hair

Ten Ways to Be an Ace Traveler

1. Take less than you think you need.
2. Listen more than you talk.
3. Expect delays.
4. Take extra money.
5. Ask, ask, ask—about everything.
6. Be kind.
7. Pay attention to detail.
8. Pray more.
9. Lend a hand.
10. Welcome surprises.

down. Or go ahead and bring your costume jewelry and gowns for a formal dinner on the town.

If you want to have a more directive experience, ask each person to come with at least one question that everyone will take turns answering. It may be something about your childhood, teen years, favorite book or movie, dream career, or top five goals to achieve before you die. Come up with suggestions for movies to rent. Try to find thought-provoking independent or foreign films no one has seen or several films with the same theme, such as *Run Lola Run* and *Sliding Doors*. These are about the meaning of the passage of time and fate in our lives, provocative topics for postmodern women on the go.

Bring photos of the most important people in your life and tell of your favorite memory with them. Bring a childhood photo of yourself and share a favorite event. For "aiding and abetting this kind of craziness," get a great little workbook by Kathleen Laing and Elizabeth Butterfield: *Girlfriends' Getaways: A Complete Guide to the Weekend Adventure That Turns Friends into Sisters and Sisters into Friends.*[2] Oh, and don't forget your camera! Several disposable cameras lying around on tables and tucked into bags mean you'll get more shots of spontaneous, silly moments. Here's to a weekend or a week that will be so inspirational you'll do it all over again year after year.

> When traveling, great teachers appear in the most unexpected ways.
>
> Will Gregory

Let's look at another context for re-creating our hectic lives. Traveling with children—now, there's a challenge. In these days of video games and automobile DVDs, traveling long distances is not as big a deal as it was just a few years ago. But it's common knowledge that watching TV, even educational programming, requires fewer brain waves than reading a book. Must a vacation with kids mean a series of movies and amusement parks? Does it mean consistent stimulation of their nervous systems with overactivity and entertainment? Can vacations with kids also be meaningful, pleasurable, and inspirational?

Pardon me for being sentimental about my upbringing in the '50s, a simpler time. My parents had little expendable income. We didn't take a vacation every year, or if we did it was just to visit relatives. Kids were not the center. But here are good things I remember about traveling in a '54 Studebaker across huge spaces of nothing on Route 66: The stunning and scary Carlsbad Caverns. Begging to try the slot machines in Nevada cafés. (Dad conceded to show us that gambling never pays, and he hit the jackpot!) How grand the Grand Canyon really is. How long it takes to drive through the Texas panhandle! Picking wild plums on a creek somewhere close to the Santa Fe Trail. Staying in funky New Mexican motels made to look like adobe haciendas. None of these things took much money. But they instilled qualities in my life that set a pattern for a positive future: families belong together, imagination is a fabulous gift, the world is a big place. I knew I wanted to see more.

Mr. Mogren was my fifth grade teacher. He had lost his right arm in the Korean War, but not one kid in the classroom thought of him as handicapped. Mr. M. could do just about anything with that stump of an arm, and sometimes he wore a hook on the end of it just to tease us. He and his wife took groups of us on camping trips in the wild. I'll never forget learning to body surf on a camping trip to the beach, looking up at the stars in Death Valley, sleeping on the sand, and learning to hike in the mountains. He taught me not to be afraid of the power of the ocean's waves but to use that power to have fun getting to shore. He wanted us to feel the earth and to experience the way the stars moved across the sky all night long. He taught us about building campfires and respecting the forests. Mr. M. was a lesson in reaching beyond my grasp. His lessons in the wilderness go way beyond nature; they're spiritual lessons for life.

I missed being able to take proper vacations with my own kids, but we did share our national heritage in the Blue Mountains and native badlands of eastern Oregon, bathe in the natural hot springs along the way, visit the Oregon Trail museum and dig clay from its muddy ruts, and camp along our state's rugged coastline. While I was envying families in our neighborhood who vacationed in Hawaii every year, I learned that their children were begging not to have to go there again. By high school, my kids were initiating their own trips and (lucky me) inviting me along. Leyah saved her money for a trip to our nation's capital instead of a trip to Cabo San Lucas with her friends for graduation; I saved mine too. We also visited prospective colleges on the East Coast. Lissa enticed me to take her to Mexico to start her volunteer work, so we drove down to the Baja Peninsula together. Tirza inspired me to join her and a roommate backpacking in

177

Europe, so I bought a plane ticket on a credit card and spent the next year paying it off.

As far as the education of children is concerned I think they should be taught not the little virtues but the great ones. Not thrift but generosity and an indifference to money; not caution but courage and a contempt for danger; not shrewdness but frankness and a love of truth; not tact but love for one's neighbor and self-denial; not a desire for success but a desire to be and to know.

Natalia Ginzburg

I like to think somehow that my kids got the travel gene from their mother and a bit of stimulation from the small, inexpensive adventures we did take: beachcombing, picnicking, art hopping, exploring backroads and cranberry bogs, visiting Christmas tree farms, and picking daffodils in wide fields of yellow. Sometimes the greatest adventure is entertaining yourself along the way: playing simple games or—gasp!—even having long conversations, an art form our society has mostly lost. Okay, I may be overly simplistic and tediously sentimental. But I like the way exploration of any kind begets itself.

For kids, vacation is another way to play. And that means seeing things from other perspectives, putting creative and critical thinking into gear. Sometimes a quiet place or the pressure of "nothing to do" is just what will bring creative urges to the surface. Allow open, white space in your family vacation; then watch what emerges and listen to everything kids don't say. Give kids permission to create their own fun in unexpected places. Offer the opportunity for physical action along with amusement of their own devising.

Sharpen observation skills along the way by recording times the sun rises and sets in different locations. Note the budding

Without Leaving Home

The alchemy of travel is much more than leaving home. It is something you can do even if you never leave town. Sometimes travel does not gad about; sometimes it just says, "I will do something to venerate the holy within myself and others." Travel without leaving your hometown. There are many options.

Volunteer. Charitable causes exist right under our noses, in the neighborhood, in local jails, in community projects. Even incarcerated women volunteer, making quilts for AIDS orphans in Africa, cleaning churches and parks, participating in Girl Scout programs. One of my friends created sack "lunches" packed with nonperishables and carried them in her car to hand out to street people. Get out of your comfort zone. Create your own travel alchemy where you live.

Run a local marathon. Support a cause like cancer research or private funding for public schools by participating in a run with thousands of other women. You'll get in shape and experience the thrill of achievement, and your donation will go toward a good cause.

Explore your hometown. Explore the downtown area of your city. Patronize old-fashioned "mom and pop" shops. Look around in back alleys and side streets to find them. Get friendly with the proprietors as you boycott corporate stores for a month or just a week. Drive into the rural areas surrounding your city. Take a walk in a place you've never been. Sketch a bridge, a dilapidated farmhouse, or a sprawling ranch. Go to local school functions even if you don't have a child there.

Write your way around. Look at your hometown as a child would. What if you had just arrived as an immigrant from a Third World country? What would it look like? How would it feel to you? Write as if you were losing your memory or eyesight and wanted to describe your hometown to a future grandchild. Wonder on paper why the streets are named as they are. Describe the landmarks of your town or memories you have of childhood places.

Meet ordinary people. Surprise yourself! Get to know at least one elderly person living at home alone. Visit a nursing home or mental health facility. Offer to mentor a woman at the local jail. Use the laundromat instead of washing clothes at home, just for the experience. Sit in a park and write stories about the people you observe. Make up vignettes about their lives.

of tree branches or kinds of fruits grown in different climates. Document the weather and sightings of birds or wildlife. What kind of clothing is necessary? Bring glue sticks and colored pencils to draw what you see and create vacation journals of leaves, flowers, and bits of nature you pick up in a park or country lane. Entertain yourselves in hotel rooms by creating pasta bracelets, crafting personalized "postcards" for friends, or serving snacks by candlelight just before bedtime.

You have only to let the place happen to you . . . the loneliness, the silence, the poverty, the futility, indeed the silliness of your life.

Kathleen Norris

Travel as adventure is way beyond going to a particular place or engaging in a particular activity, sport, or challenge. It includes what might otherwise be considered the mundane, the relaxing, the responsible: girlfriend getaways, travels with children, even business trips. Creating a life pattern of adventure means we include these things as ways to embrace the abundant life in all its kaleidoscopic patterns and nuances of color.

Adventure is a way to open pastures, to feed on what nourishes us, inspires others, energizes our gifts, and puts us in touch with God. Never underestimate where the abundant life may take you: serving on a mission trip to Cuba or Jamaica, attending an inspiring concert on a business trip, snowboarding in the Rockies, camping with a group of young people in the wilderness, sharing tea and your life with a girlfriend at Starbucks. Your life counts. Be sure you get—and give—all the adventure you can.

Unpacking Chernobyl

A Pilgrim's Profile: Beth Lueders

How I learned to see faraway people not
as statistics but as my next door
neighbors

I soon realized that no journey carries one far unless, as it extends into the world around us, it goes an equal distance into the world within.

Lillian Smith

W hat can we do?" That was the question posed by a New York City pastor when in July of 1990 the Soviet government finally asked for help four years after the Chernobyl explosion. Beth Lueders, a journalist whose work has taken her to seventeen countries, was one whose presence was part of the answer to that question. Beth, of Colorado Springs, joined others on a humanitarian trip the following year sponsored by the Byelorussian Children's Fund. Their mission was to visit hospitals and clinics, bringing boxes of medical supplies—basic equipment the Soviets could not get—and expensive cancer medicine. Unpacked throughout the trip were also toys, Bibles, and love.

"The people were thrilled that we would travel across the world just to help them," Beth says. But she adds that travel also benefits the one who goes. "It gives you a bigger picture of what God is doing and an understanding who God is. He is so much bigger than our sanitized Western world."

Along the Ukraine border, Beth saw children lying in cage-like cribs at an orphanage where those born with birth defects had been abandoned by their parents. Children were especially susceptible to the leakage of radiation at Chernobyl. After the explosion of the nuclear reactor, thyroid disease and birth defects doubled. Anemia increased seven times. Chronic illness of the nose and throat were almost tenfold, with other illnesses expected to take at least twenty years to show up.

Beth says, "In the Chernobyl area, fruit trees are withered black. Mothers don't know how to stop their children's bleeding noses. I knew we couldn't just say, 'Jesus loves you.' I wondered how God was going to use me and use what I was experiencing there."

Touring the thirty kilometer contaminated zone in a decades-old, small bus, Beth met one family who refused to move even though the radiation readings were still extremely high. "They lived in denial," she says, adding, "I don't want to be in denial. I'm not a tragedy queen, but anytime you get outside the continental United States, it makes you grateful. I came back a changed person."

Among the most touching of Beth's experiences was attending a government-sanctioned Russian Orthodox Christmas service in the Minsk Russian Orthodox Cathedral. For seventy-three years—since 1917—Communist rule forbade the Russian people from worshiping in public. "It was an emotional thing to be part of that," Beth admits. "In our country, we often go to church as if in a state of boredom, or we blow it off altogether if we're tired that day. For these people standing—not sitting—in a sanctuary lit only by candlelight, worship together was tremendously meaningful. Their service includes many icons, and the people kiss them with great respect and devotion.

"I'm not a complainer or a whiner," Beth continues, "but I've been humbled at what goes on behind the scenes in the lives of people all over the world. It is while traveling—whether in the Congo, the Philippines, Puerto Rico, Greece, Hungary, or England—that I've learned to see people not as statistics but as human lives with something to teach. Most people in other countries do not have the necessities we have, let alone the conveniences. They don't have the inspirational books, music, and conferences so plentiful in our culture. But I've found people of other cultures tremendously generous. They have a joyful, authentic faith that is not based on circumstances.

"We need to get outside our comfort zones in order to get outside our egocentric mindset," Beth insists. "For me, it was not just wondering whether to shower in the polluted water in Minsk," she says. "It was not just balking at brushing my teeth with that water. Back home again, I'm grateful for what I have, but I face the questions. How will I use what I've experienced overseas with my next door neighbor who is an amputee? How will I share it with a friend who is struggling with breast cancer?

"I've seen many suffering people wherever I've been," Beth says. "I've taken dirty, starving children on my lap. I've sensed something of what Jesus felt when the crowds of people pressed close to him. As a journalist, I am usually trying to stay neutral in order to tell the story, but all the while I am fighting back tears. For me, the issue is compassion. At home again, I want to live that out. My trip often begins when I return to my own hometown."

183

12

The Great Romance

An Epilogue

All the great travel books are love stories, by some reckoning—
from the Odyssey and the Aeneid to the Divine Comedy and
the New Testament—and all good trips are, like love, about being
carried out of yourself and deposited in the midst of terror and
wonder.

Pico Iyer

Ah, honeymoons. The ultimate pilgrimage.

Having never experienced a honeymoon does not leave
me in a good position to write about them. The week before
my 1974 wedding, our destination in the California mountains
experienced a forest fire. We arrived to a blackened landscape.
The cabin we'd reserved had survived. It stood waiting for us in
an otherwise otherworldly moonscape.

This was, of course, a strong metaphor, although I didn't know
it then—a sign of portending disaster just like the borrowed

wedding getaway car that wouldn't start on cue and the traffic ticket my groom garnered once it finally did. Our week in the Idyll Wild was a romantic disaster. And yet . . .

There are so many honeymoons in life. As I think back, just about every trip I've ever taken has been one, or has become one in the process. That's because I fell in love on every trip I've ever taken.

I fell in love with the beautiful French-Afro children in Haiti. I wanted to take every one of them home with me, feed them, swathe them in soft blankets, and tuck them into bed with hugs and kisses.

I fell in love with the stone out of which Jerusalem is built, an incredible sandy color like the deserts, shining gold in the lights upon the walls of the old city at night. No wonder they call it "Jerusalem, the Gold."

I fell in love with the deep blue sea of Mexico, where the water was warm and awash with light. In a little out-of-the-way village called Bara de Navidad, long past Puerto Vallarta, the local community enlivened the streets with chatter. Weathered faces and wonderful native families, not tourists, characterized the tiny ancient trading port that jutted into the Pacific. Compared to Anyplace, USA, we'd call them poor, but they were not.

Honeymoons, you see, happen when you travel, even when you're alone. That is, honeymoons happen when you travel if you follow your heart. They happen when travel as pilgrimage and adventure becomes woven with your journey of spiritual and personal growth. When adventure gets in your life blood, working its way into the cells of your body, you can't *not* travel. You become a sojourner, never again to look at the world through the eyes of a tourist. Like Alice found when she peered through the looking glass, everything you experience becomes not ordinary. You'll never go back to business as usual. You're trapped in the Great Romance.

Before You Leave

Make your list and check it twice. Here's what to remember before you leave for the airport or train station or pull your car out of the garage for that cross-country trip:

- Are you wearing your driver's license, passport, and tickets? They should be ensconced somewhere on your body.
- Did you say one last good-bye to children, parents, spouse, or best friend?
- Are you sure you really want to take that extra pair of shoes? (You'll be sorry.)
- Check once more that you grabbed your makeup bag and toothbrush off the bathroom counter.
- You did ask your neighbor to pick up the mail, didn't you?
- Is the coffeemaker turned off? Are all the windows locked tight?
- Where is that extra film you just bought for the camera?

Lock the door behind you. Take a deep breath. Be present with yourself.

A man's life is nothing but an extended trek through the detours of art to recapture those one or two moments when his heart first opened.

Albert Camus

When travel becomes romance, people are no longer just people. They are prophetic souls who offer messages about who you are and why you are here. Their eyes and smiles will intoxicate you. Ordinary human beings become vibrant and radiant, because you suddenly see why we need each other. Local people seen through the eyes of romance will light up your world like candles glimmering in a honeymoon suite. They'll fill you with happy wonder as if you're sitting under a palm cabana and Pacific stars. When you get back to the stay-at-home, workaday world, there will no doubt be a lingering glow.

Now, this is not to say that all your experiences with people will be pleasant ones or that it's easy to interact with foreign cultures whose national personality is very different from your own. I've met my share of rude, upsetting, and difficult locals. But when experienced in the context of adventure, irritating and annoying qualities are less grating. They are assuaged by your own appreciation for and acceptance of people exactly as they are.

I saw such a lingering glow when my youngest daughter, Lissa, returned from an impoverished and rumpled village in Baja where she worked at an orphanage. Sleeping in the nursery with the babies, she had to get up frequently to change diapers, rock restless little bodies, and calm toddlers who woke with bad dreams. It was a brutal schedule. The nursery was primitive—not pastel and filled with soft things the way a nursery should be. Nothing had been painted or spruced up. There were few lotions or baby supplies. Few toys or fuzzy clothes. The rooms had no heat source and remained chilled from the spring rains. Breakfast, lunch, and dinner consisted invariably of beans and rice. Longer-term volunteers treated Lissa with indifference. But when she returned home to our cozy Oregon town, she was literally shining. There was a light and glitter in her eyes and skin that was unmistakable. Her school guidance counselor asked me, "Is Lissa glowing, or is that just her tan?" I thought I was the only one who noticed.

True romance is when the siren call of adventure changes you forever. It is when your travels start changing you, and others notice. For those who don't write, all travel finally becomes spiritual travel, because travel ultimately is a spiritual experience. For writers who travel, the genre of spiritual travel writing is ultimately what all writing becomes. But even writers don't really write about travel. In reality, travel writes you. It inscribes itself on your soul. It dictates, changes, and rattles your everyday. You

Romantic Getaways for Two

When heading off on a getaway with your spouse, you don't need to spend a wad to enjoy the feeling of Paris or Casablanca.

Choose a beautiful natural place for daytime excursions. Share a gourmet picnic on a hilltop with a view. Walk in a meadow filled with wildflowers—bring a small blanket to sit on, cheese, bread, and a bottle of sparkling water. Relax on a sandy beach—bring sand forms for making dream castles. Take a hike along mountain streams or around lakes; look for covered bridges, old barns, waterfalls. Walk along an ocean or lake coastline; build a fire on a beach or campground and bring wooly blankets to wrap up in. Sip warm cocoa.

Make any room a second honeymoon boudoir. Bring several candles in votive jars (don't forget matches) and a small CD player to create your own glow. Take along a soft, pretty-colored throw for silky cuddling before bedtime. Pack a cute basket with exotic snacks from a foreign market, your favorite drinks, and a couple of china plates or crystal glasses and cloth napkins. Don't forget your favorite scented body oil or lotion for massages. Fuzzy slippers saved for special occasions are oh so sensual. A must: your sexiest underwear!

Create your own entertainment. Visit small towns in out of the way places or the countryside. Amuse yourselves in local boutiques, wineries, historic museums, gardens and parks, or swimming spots. Visit cities and check out the high-end areas where the swanky people shop. Get sushi to go and eat it in the park. Get lost in specialty boutiques and bookstores. Listen to music in the best CD stores; share your favorites with each other. Pick out new music for road trips. See vintage movies at retro theaters or foreign films at small local venues. Or rent the movies you didn't get around to seeing last year and snuggle in the hotel room amid piles of pillows. Go to the nearest beach town and play the games at a seaside arcade. Buy fudge. Stroll along the boardwalk. Sit in the sun and watch the other couples.

Just for fun. Take lots of pictures of yourselves together. These turn out fun just by extending the camera in one hand and holding it out to shoot the photo (smile!). Write love letters to each other on fancy stationery with fancy pens. Read your favorite story, favorite jokes, or favorite poetry to each other in bed. Create a wish jar by each writing out a hundred wishes for your life together on small slips of paper. Roll them up and drop them into a glass vase or pretty jar. Pick one out each day or week to read together over the following months. Bring out the CD player and spin the platters to create a mood of frolic or tenderness as you turn out the light. Dance naked if you dare.

keep the pen flowing, the keys clicking, just to keep up, but you never really can keep up. When a sense of place invades your inner territory, you can never capture the true romance of it all. You start out by sensing with eyes and ears and touch, and you end up experiencing life through another, more authentic kind of sensual authority.

I envisage life to be given so that we may stitch the worlds back up without the seam showing. That is what a sacred journey can do. Stitching needs the thread to go in and out, up and down; and since those first journeys, I have followed the thread wherever it has taken me.

Roger Housden

"A good wine tastes like a grape," a winegrower once told my sweetheart and me. It was on a rainy day in a rustic little wine room in what seemed like the middle of nowhere. He added, "A great wine tastes like a place."

His statement stopped us cold. This guy had sold his place in Napa Valley, California, because the business had become too commercial there. He'd moved to the green rolling hills of southern Oregon and bought the oldest winery in the state, a place much like Napa had been forty years before. Down to earth. Quiet. Rich in soil rather than profit. Arriving in his work clothes and with paint-spattered hands, he told of working the land, explaining how most wineries profit on young wines, two to three years old, bottled and sold as premium wines. As a wine neophyte, I was fascinated as he explained how wine from vines less than ten years old isn't worthy to be consumed. He offered us samples of wine from a fourteen-year-old vine, and we compared it to the other wines we'd tasted that day from young vines.

"It's all in the complexity," he said. Although we are not experienced connoisseurs, we immediately experienced what he meant. The taste of the old wine from the old vineyard was beyond anything I'd tasted anywhere.

Since then, I've thought a lot about the idea that a good wine tastes like a grape, while a great wine tastes like a place. I've turned it over and over in my mind, wondering how this relates to who I am, to the places by which I've been influenced. I've thought about the transient culture we live in, how the average person moves every two to three years, and why I'm captivated by the people groups who are rooted and grounded in a sense of place for a much longer time. Their lives change mine, because, like great wines, it's all in the complexity. When you taste the difference, you stop tasting and sampling; you buy a bottle of the good stuff.

Spiritual adventure and pilgrimage is bliss without being blissed-out, because it takes you somewhere and changes you. As Pico Iyer says, every journey can be a love affair: "You're left puzzling over who you are and whom you've fallen in with. . . . And if travel is like love, it is, in the end, because it admits us to a heightened state of awareness . . . ready to be transformed."[1]

Travel has taken me on many a honeymoon time after time. Each time I go, I encounter a place that promises I will never be the same. Neither will the places where I've left my heart. When I returned from Haiti, I wrote a magazine article about what I had seen so briefly and the impressions the place and its people had left on me. An accompanying piece told of the orphans I had met and their beautiful lives amid squalor and hunger and lack of everything Americans consider necessary to survival. Years later, at a conference in another state halfway across our continent, I met a woman at dinner one night who said, "Oh, you're Marlee?" She continued without a smile, "Well, you ruined my life!"

I was stunned and speechless.

Armchair Travel
for the Pilgrims at Home

Can't get enough travel—and can't seem to get up and go? With what's on the screen in your own home, you can still find the transforming experience of new people and places.

First stop: the Internet. The wonders of the World Wide Web can offer nourishment for the spirit, ideas for the mind to wrestle with, poetry to feed the soul, and people to meet. Travel, of course, implies missing someone or something left behind just as it implies meeting someone new or being someplace you never knew existed. Yet, in virtual pilgrimage, you escape the sweet sorrow of separation. Surround yourself with maps and books about the places you want to go. Just reading about a place or seeing photos of it will take you somewhere. Today I visited Constantinople because after talking with a friend about Byzantine crosses, I got to wondering where the Byzantine Empire really was. Curiosity has a power that transcends place.

Next stop: film! Movies can take you places you've never been and immerse you in an experience there. I love movies about women who have an adventure. Here are just a few of my favorites that have taken me around the world:

- *Casablanca* with Ingrid Bergman, takes place in Morocco
- *River Queen* with Katherine Hepburn, takes place in Africa
- *The Sound of Music* with Julie Andrews, takes place in Salzburg, Austria
- *Out of Africa* with Meryl Streep, takes place in Kenya
- *Agnes Brown* with Anjelica Huston, takes place in Ireland
- *Chocolat* with Juliette Binoche, takes place in France
- *Like Water for Chocolate* with Lumi Cavazos, takes place in Mexico
- *Hideous Kinky* with Kate Winslet, takes place in Katmandu, Nepal
- *The River Wild* with Meryl Streep, takes place in the American wilderness
- *The English Patient* with Kristin Scott Thomas, takes place in the Middle East
- *The Mask*, a film about a little girl's friendship with an old man, takes place in China
- *The Red Violin* with various actors, takes place all over the world

Even in virtual travel, you stop being a spectator. You engage your own life. You can sit down to conversation at one of the many websites for thinkers and wanderers or talk with friends in a faraway place about a movie. Do some mental traveling and celebrate every minute of it. It is the sense of place you bring to the screen (your computer or TV) that counts. To study places through media is a chance for the lame to walk.

"You wrote that article about Haiti," she said, "and it ruined me. I couldn't sleep at night. You see, I have three children of my own, but I just had to go down there and adopt another child. Look, here's his picture!" The woman dug into her purse and pulled out a photo of an adorable little boy surrounded by his white brothers and sister, all of them smiling ear to ear. "You ruined me for living the status quo," she told me. "And I have never been so happy!"

Travel changed me, and through me it changed the life of someone else. Everybody will find a different, personal way to live out adventure and make of it a great wine. If you haven't had a honeymoon in a while, isn't it about time?

Notes

Start Packing

1. Michael McGirr, *Things You Get For Free* (New York: Atlantic Monthly Press, 2002), 14.

2. Phil Cousineau, *The Art of Pilgrimage* (Berkeley: Canari Press, 1998), xix–xx.

3. Ibid., xiv.

Chapter 1: HerStory

1. Marybeth Bond, "Women Travel Statistics," Women Travel Tips, 2004, www.womentraveltips.com/stats.shtml.

2. Genesis 16:13.

3. 1 Samuel 25:14–35.

4. Anna G. Edmonds, *Turkey's Religious Sites* (Istanbul: Damko Publications, 1997), 61–65, 145.

5. Julia Bolton Holloway, "Helena, Egeria and Paula: The Bible and Women Pilgrims," Melting Pot Fortune City, 1997, www.meltingpot.fortunecity.com/Ukraine/324/egeria.html.

6. Ruth Tucker and Walter Liefeld, "Wed Only to Their Master," Mission Frontiers, www.missionfrontiers.org/1999/08/single.html. Excerpted from *Daughters of the Church* (Grand Rapids: Zondervan, 1987).

7. Ibid.

8. Milbry Polk and Mary Tiegreen, *Women of Discovery: A Celebration of Intrepid Women Who Explored the World* (New York: Clarkson Potter, 2001).

9. Whitney Otto, *How to Make an American Quilt* (New York: Ballantine Books, 1991), 129.

Chapter 2: A Holy Calling

1. Song of Solomon 1:4.

2. Song of Solomon 7:11–12.

Chapter 3: God's Outward Bound School

1. Phil Cousineau, "Introduction to Pilgrimage," www.travelerstales.com/catalog/pilgrimage/intro.html. Excerpted from *Adventures of the Spirit*, ed. Sean O'Reilly and James O'Reilly (San Francisco: Traveler's Tales, 2000).

2. Ibid.

3. Martin Buber, *I and Thou*, trans. Walter Kaufmann (New York: Simon & Schuster, 1996), 67–68.

Chapter 4: Mapping Your Terrain

1. J. R. R. Tolkien, *The Fellowship of the Ring* in James B. Simpson, *Simpson's Contemporary Quotations* (Boston: Houghton Mifflin, 1988), Bartleby.com, 2000, www.bartleby.com/63/98/5398.html.

2. Robyn Davidson, *Tracks: Solo Trek Across Australia's Outback* (New York: Pantheon, 1980; First Vintage Books Edition, 1995), 120.

3. Isaiah 45:15.

4. Oliver Cromwell, "Essays in English History, Cromwell and the Historians" in A. J. P. Taylor, *The Columbia World of Quotations* (New York: Columbia University Press, 1996), Bartleby.com, 2001, www.bartleby.com/66/88/15418.html.

Chapter 5: Condition the Soles of Your Soul

1. Jon Kabat-Zinn, "You Can't Stop the Waves but You Can Learn to Surf," *Wherever You Go There You Are* (Westport, CT: Hyperion Press, 1995), 265.

2. Elizabeth Barrett Browning, "Quotes," www.home.utm.net/pan/quotes.html.

3. Pico Iyer, *Falling Off the Map* (New York: Alfred A. Knopf, 1993), 91.

4. Kelly Winters, "Trusting the Trail," *A Woman's Path*, ed. Lucy McCauley, Amy G. Carlson, and Jennifer Leo (San Francisco: Travelers' Tales, 2000), 241.

5. Barbara Sjoholm, "Halibut Woman," *A Woman Alone*, ed. Faith Conlon, Ingrid Emerick, and Christina Henry de Tessan (Seattle: Seal Press, 2001), 27, 39.

6. *Alive*, Touchstone and Paramount, prod. Robert Watts, 1993. From the book by Piers Paul Read.

7. Terry Tempest Williams, *An Unspoken Hunger* (New York: Vintage Books, 1994), *New York Times* quote on front flap.

8. Sjoholm, "Halibut Woman," *A Woman Alone*, 41.

9. Joanna L. Stratton, *Pioneer Women: Voices trom the Kansas Frontier* (New York: Simon & Schuster, 1981), 112.

10. Song of Solomon 7:1.

11 Cousineau, "Introduction to Pilgrimage."

12. Deuteronomy 29:5.

13. Isaiah 52:7.

14. Revelation 10:1.

Chapter 6: Respect the Unexpected

1. A. K. M. Adam, "The Pilgrimage of Etheria," www.ccel.org/m/mcclure/etheria/etheria.htm. Excerpted from M. S. McClure and C. L. Feltoe, D.D., ed and trans., *The Pilgrimage of Etheria* (London: Society for Promoting Christian Knowledge, 1919).

2. Paula McDonald, "Unexpected Trails" (a sidebar), in *A Woman's World*, ed. Marybeth Bond (San Francisco: Travelers' Tales, 1995), 361.

3. "Notable Kansas Women," Kansas State Historical Society, 2004, www.kshs.org/people/women.htm.

4. Thomas Moore, *The Soul of Sex, Cultivating Life as an Act of Love* (New York: HarperCollins, 1998), 276.

5. Susan Harrow, *Sell Yourself without Selling Your Soul* (New York: HarperResource, 2002), 328.

6. Polk and Tiegreen, *Women of Discovery*.

Chapter 7: A Woman's Perspective

1. Bond, *A Woman's World*, xvi.

2. Holly Morris, "Women's Travel Takes Off," www.archive.abcnews.com/sections/business/biztravl/28/sidetrips.com.

3. Diana Webb, "Women Pilgrims of the Middle Ages," Volume 48, Issue 7, *History Today*, July 1998, www.findarticles.com/p/articles/mi_m1373/is_n7_v48/ai_20964199.

4. Davidson, *Tracks*, 238.

5. St. Therese Couderc, "Meet St. Therese Couderc," Religion of the Cenacle, 2001, www.cenaclesisters.org/stcouderc.htm.

Chapter 8: The Mystique of Thin Places

1. Alain de Botton, *The Art of Travel* (New York: Pantheon, 2002), 56.

2. *Grand Canyon*, Twentieth Century Fox, prod. Lawrence Kasdan, 1992.

3. John O'Donohue, Anam Cara, as quoted at Riley and Riley, "Walking in Thin Places," 2004, www.riley-photography.com/walking.html.

4. Peter Gomes, "Words for the Heart," David Gergen's Essays and Dialogues, December 25, 1996, www.pbs.org/newshour/gergen.

5. Sir Thomas Browne, Religio Medici, The First Part, Section II at Under the Sun, www.underthesun.cc/classics/Browne/ReligioMedici/ReligioMedici3.html.

6. Mark Twain, *The Innocents Abroad*, chapter LXII, *The Complete Works of Mark Twain*, n.d., www.mtwain.com/Innocents_Abroad/63/html.

7. Robert Lewis Stevenson, "Robert Lewis Stevenson's Famous Quotes," 1996, www.thinkexist.com/English/Author/t/Author_3988_1.htm.

8. Edward Reed, *The Necessity of Experience* (New Haven: Yale University Press, 1996), 5.

Chapter 9: Mission Possible

1. Joy Broyles Yohay, "Five Pounds of Almonds," *A Woman's World*, ed. Marybeth Bond, 3–11.

2. Bond, *A Woman's World*, xxiii.

3. Julian of Norwich, "Revelations of Divine Love," Enlightening Messages, 2004, www.enlightening messages.org/inspirational quotes.html.

4. Faith Conlon, Ingrid Emerick, Christina Henry de Tessan, eds., *A Woman Alone* (Seattle: Seal Press, 2001), x.

5. Henry David Thoreau, *Walden*, Classic Reader, 2004, www.classicreader.com/read.php/sid.1/bookid.108/sec.18.

6. Myrna Grant, *Sacred Legacy* (Grand Rapids: Baker, 2003), 116.

7. Don Miguel Ruiz, *The Four Agreements* (Berkeley: Amber-Allen, 1997), xvi.

Chapter 10: Travel Alchemy

1. Oliver Wendell Holmes Jr., Rand Lindsly's *Quotations*, the Quotations Page, 2004, www.quotationspage.com.

2. Frank MacEowen, *The Mist-Filled Path: Celtic Wisdom for Exiles, Wanderers and Seekers* (Novato, CA: New World Library, 2002), 235.

3. Freya Stark, "Baghdad Sketches," 1933; Brothers Judd, 2004, www. brothersjudd.com/index.cfm/fuseaction/reviews.detail/book_is/1194/Baghdad%20Sket.htm.

4. Shelly Friesen Hawkins, *Student Travel Magazine*, Summer 1998, 58.

5. MacEowen, *The Mist-Filled Path*, 235.

6. Matthew 8:22.

7. Matthew 10:8, 16.

8. James Joyce, in Gibbs A. Williams, Ph.D., "Some Seminal Books That Have Aided My Search for the Good Life," 2004, www.gibbsonline.com/gibbsbooks.html.

9. Ernest Hemingway, quoted in *The New Yorker*, 2004, www.geocities. com/Athens/Oracle/6517/courage.htm.

10. Martha Sherrill, "Walk On the Wild Side," *AARP*, Nov/Dec 2003, 38–43.

11. Ursula LeGuin, Wisdom Quotes, www.wisdomquotes.com.002614. html.

Chapter 11: Furious Faith in Forward Motion

1. John 10:9–10.

2. Kathleen Laing and Elizabeth Butterfield, *Girlfriends' Getaways* (Colorado Springs: Waterbrook Press, 2002).

Chapter 12: The Great Romance

1. Pico Iyer, *Falling in Love with the World*, adapted from *Los Angeles Times* magazine, "Why We Travel," Beliefnet.com, August 3, 2003, www.beliefnet. com/story/126/story_12639_1.html.

Acknowledgments

This book is offered with a grateful heart to the people who have sponsored some of my trips abroad—Food for the Hungry, the Israeli Ministry of Tourism and that of Turkey—and to people who sustained me in far-off places: my father, who sent checks at random when I was living on tea and fruit in Jerusalem; the Bathman and Bounds families at the Rosenhof in Salzburg, along with Helen and Les, who never complained about my cooking; and the folks at Sylvia Beach Hotel in Newport, Oregon, where I met dozens of savvy travelers with amazing stories.

To my sister, Carol, thank you for insisting I join you for a first ever trip abroad (it changed my life), and to my firstborn, Tirza, for inviting me to don a backpack twenty-five years later and revisit those places with you.

I owe much gratitude to people who inspired and comforted me when it seemed I lost my way in oh so many places: Paul, you kept me laughing in Rome. Jimmy, you were there—surprise!—when my plane arrived late in London's unfriendly rain. Jane, you served me countless cups of tea by your crackling English fire. Trevor, you were my prayer partner when things got tough at Greenwoods. Mary, you inspired me by your courage as you tackled life on the road, a young widow with a baby boy. John and Elizabeth, you taught me to see like a writer. Joyce, you were my dearest "cistern" all over the Holy Land. My family in Denmark, you offered "hygge" and warmth during my twelve-year sojourn there. Mom, you never begged me to come home; you gave me wings.

To the travelers extraordinaire, Leyah and Lissa, go profound respect for the way you picked up the pieces and moved on with me in a new direction when the way back was no longer an option. To Jeanette, Kelley, and the people at Revell for their professional vision and the guidance they've lavished upon this project, my deep appreciation. To all my fellow pilgrims, those many unnamed, thank you for the sacred journeys.

Marlee LeDai . . .

is an author of more than twenty-five books. As an editor and writer, she has contributed to many more, including *Keeper of the Springs* with Ingrid Trobisch; Tyndale's *The Family Bible*; Focus on the Family's *Caring for Aging Loved Ones*; and books by Barbara Johnson.

With her third infant on her knee, Marlee translated the stories of Hans Christian Andersen from old-world Danish into English—and contributed to other best-selling editions (more than 7 million books sold). Her children's book *Grandpa and Me: We Learn About Death* received the C. S. Lewis Gold Medallion Award.

Marlee was editor and columnist of *Virtue* magazine and a contributing editor to *Aspire* magazine. Writing for a variety of other magazines and online sites, she's published more than 150 articles, cover stories, and interviews. She teaches on the spiritual voices of women at Writers.com, and she helped launch two websites: the American Bible Society's ForMinistry.com, and Damarisproject. org, sponsored by the Damaris Project, which seeks to nurture faith in America's educated professional women.

Marlee is on the executive board of Freedom in the Son, Inc., a ministry to incarcerated women serving Oregon's female inmates. She is a spiritual director, trained by the Art of Sacred Living Center in Bend, Oregon. Speaking about making a house a home, travel, and life pilgrimage, she leads workshops for women in transition and serves as a mentor on moving forward.

With an eye on stories that offer healing and inspiration, Marlee has lived and worked in a variety of places abroad, including Francis and Edith Schaeffer's L'Abri community in the Swiss Alps. As a journalist, she's traveled widely in Israel (between the Munich massacre and the Yom Kippur War); behind the Iron Curtain (during the Cold War); to Haiti (during the U.S. embargo); through Turkey's religious sites; and along Normandy's D-Day trail, interviewing both locals and American veterans for the anniversary celebration.

Marlee's love of family, adventure, and women's culture characterize her life. Now a grandmother, she enjoys hiking, fly fishing, and snowboarding in the Pacific Northwest.

Leyah Jensen . . .

is a book designer for Scholastic and lives in the East Village of New York City. In her spare time, she writes and illustrates.

As the daughter of author Marlee LeDai, Leyah was taught the joys of travel early in life. She has been to Europe often, sometimes sleeping in train stations when her budget ran out with the plane ticket, yet she feels most fulfilled by visiting developing countries. Leyah has reported on the slums of the Dominican Republic and has taught art to orphans in Haiti. In each new city, she documents her experience in words and drawings. Leyah keeps her belongings few beyond a camera, a laptop, and her journals. That way, she's always prepared for a journey.

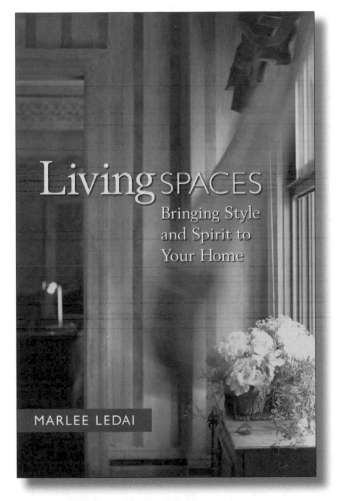